IRRESISTIBLE CHANGE GUIDE™

By
Heather Stagl

IRRESISTIBLE CHANGE GUIDE: DESIGN & INFLUENCE CHANGE WITHOUT GETTING STUCK
© 2014 by Enclaria LLC
ISBN: 978-0-692-22362-8

All rights reserved. No part of this document or the related files may be reproduced or transmitted in any form, by any means (electronic, photocopying, or otherwise) without the prior written permission of the publisher.

This document is intended for personal use only. If you are a consultant or training provider interested in using the Irresistible Change Guide™ as part of your services, or if you are building an internal change methodology and would like to incorporate all or part of the Irresistible Change Guide™ into your approach, please contact Enclaria LLC for bulk pricing or licensing.

This publication is designed to provide accurate and authoritative information in regard to the subject matter. It is sold with the understanding that the author is not engaged in rendering a professional service. The author disclaims any responsibility or liability resulting from actions advocated or discussed in this book.

This publication was originally published as IRRESISTIBLE: THE CHANGE AGENT'S GUIDE TO DESIGN AND INFLUENCE CHANGE WITHOUT GETTING STUCK, © 2012 by Enclaria LLC. The "Gain Leadership Support" chapter was adapted from BEYOND BUY-IN: RAISE LEADERSHIP SUPPORT FOR YOUR CHANGE INITIATIVE, © 2009 by Enclaria LLC. The "Pinpoint Communication" chapter was adapted from PINPOINT COMMUNICATION: PLAN TO AVOID SCATTERSHOT CHANGE, © 2009 by Monica Nakielski and Heather Stagl.

For information please contact:
Enclaria LLC
12850 Hwy 9 Suite 600-237
Alpharetta, GA 30004
www.enclaria.com

Dear Change Agent,

Thank you so much for choosing to make a difference at work. By opening this workbook, you have already shown a commitment to making an impact that will help you and your change initiative become *Irresistible*.

After years of working with change agents and having been an internal change agent myself for many years, I have observed that change is change, no matter what type of initiative you are implementing. At Enclaria, I work with people in roles within such diverse areas as human resources, information technology, project management, sustainability, strategic planning, and engineering, and I continue to be amazed at the similarity in the challenges that arise and in how we have successfully approached change together.

My clients say the best thing about working with me is, "You help me get unstuck." It is with the intention of helping more change agents to not only become unstuck, but to not get stuck in the first place, that I have documented my approach to change in *Irresistible Change Guide: Design and Influence Change Without Getting Stuck*.

No, there is no one-size-fits-all solution to change. However, there are fundamental ways to work through your initiative that can help you clarify, design, and influence change. No matter where you are in your initiative, the *Irresistible Change Guide* workbook will walk you through each of those elements to either get you started, keep you moving, or get unstuck.

You will notice I use the word "we" a lot in this workbook, as if I were right beside you while you are filling it out. I hope you will see we are in this together. If at any time you do get stuck or have a question, please do not hesitate to call or email me.

May your change initiative and your influence be truly *Irresistible*.

Best regards,

Heather Stagl
Enclaria LLC
(678) 644-2886
heather@enclaria.com

COMPLETE YOUR TOOLKIT
WITH E-TEMPLATES AND MORE

at

www.enclaria.com/ICGtemplates

Table of Contents

Introduction   i

1. Clarity

Assess Reality   3

Define the Future   15

Clarify the Change   25

Uncover Resistance   39

2. Leadership

Assign Roles & Relationships   57

Gain Leadership Support   69

3. Structural Influence

Structural Influence   87

Ensure Accountability   95

Pinpoint Communication   107

4. Personal Influence

Personal Influence   125

Boost Your Power   131

Start Conversations   139

Facilitate Meetings   151

Appendix   161

Introduction

About This Workbook

The *Irresistible Change Guide* is a resource for change agents – individuals working within organizations who influence others to change the way they work. The role of a change agent is a difficult one; leading change from the middle of an organization means having responsibility for making the change happen without the direct authority to get it done. Driving change from the middle takes a combination of change know-how and courage.

In my experience working with change agents like yourself, I have found that clarity breeds confidence, and in turn, confidence enables influence. This workbook contains tools for clarifying many of the moving parts of change. It organizes the different pieces, and also saves you time by providing charts, templates and checklists. But mostly, it helps you get clear about your initiative and illuminates what to do next.

While the exercises in this workbook can be completed by the change agent alone, they are meant to be completed with the people who are leading and going through the change, with the exception of the Personal Influence section. Involving others in designing the change will go a long way towards gaining buy-in and engagement.

First, let's talk about how change initiatives can get stuck. Next, we'll discuss the underlying principles of this workbook and how they prevent your change from getting stuck. Then, you'll get a preview of what you will accomplish when you complete this workbook.

How Change Gets Stuck

The path to implementing change in an organization isn't always smooth. On the way, you run into frequent speed bumps, wrong way signs, and even concrete barriers. These road hazards on the way to change act as obstacles that prevent you from moving forward. In a word, you and your change initiative get stuck.

Consider the following ten reasons your change may be stuck in a rut – or signs you may be about to lose traction.

1. Getting Off to a False Start
As a change agent, it is easy to want to jump in and start moving. But before you can start changing the organization, you must understand the organization as it is now. Organizations that jump to solutions before understanding the problem are bound to find that the problem still lingers, even after the initiative has been implemented.

2. Focus on Implementation

Sometimes you can get so caught up in implementing the initiative that the implementation becomes the end goal, instead of creating an actual change. The end result of change should never be the installation of something new; the installation must cause the organization to move towards the desired end result, or vision. Organizations that lose sight of the vision end up celebrating implementation of an initiative that doesn't actually cause the organization to change.

3. Only Scratching the Surface

Usually, what you think needs to change is not the whole story. You need to understand the real transitions involved that go deeper than the surface process or organization that is changing. If the surface system changes while underlying behaviors and mindsets remain the same, you'll see people going through the motions without actually incorporating the changes into the way they work.

4. Overcoming Resistance

What we often call resistance – procrastination, stonewalling, ignoring, etc. – is really just a symptom of something else going on. When you try to overcome the symptoms of resistance, you usually end up with more resistance. After all, resistance is a label we use as a change agent when people don't do what we expect. The instinct to hesitate and remain in control is a natural reaction people have when faced with change. To influence change, you have to uncover and work with the real sources of resistance to help people move beyond them.

5. Lack of Visible, Consistent Leadership Support

While change doesn't have to start at the top, at some point leaders who have authority in the organization must demonstrate support for the change to those who follow. Support includes not just verbal buy-in but a commitment to do what it takes to implement the change. Inconsistency in communication, decisions, accountability, and the like undermines the change effort and signals that people shouldn't take the project too seriously. Without leadership support, your change at best will fizzle out.

6. Allowing Excuses

People are busy. They don't have a big enough budget. Something unforeseeable happens. Or things are out of their control. There are a number of seemingly good reasons that people can come up with for why change isn't happening. But change gets stuck when people are allowed to not follow through and when excuses are acceptable reasons for not getting things done. Without real accountability, the organization is just spinning its wheels.

7. Scattershot Communication

Communicating is one of the main things change agents do to drive change. But it's not enough to have a lot of communication – although if you aren't communicating enough, the message will get lost in the day-to-day work. You must also make sure people are hearing the message that they need to hear, and that they do something with it. Scattershot communication is ignored, is misunderstood, or causes confusion.

8. Death by Meeting
Meetings are the default way things get done in groups in most organizations. And change is no exception. Sometimes meetings are reduced to going through the motions, and nothing happens in between them to move change forward. If your meetings are on autopilot, your change is probably stuck in meeting limbo.

9. Undiscussables
Organizations have topics that seem undiscussable – things everyone knows about except the person who could do something about it. But some uncomfortable topics must be approached during change, such as leadership behaviors, uncovering resistance, and providing feedback. When behaviors or other obstacles that prevent change go unaddressed because silence is easier, it becomes impossible to move forward. After all, you can't fix what no one will admit exists.

10. Limited Personal Influence
When you are the main torchbearer for your change initiative, the project may have trouble expanding beyond the boundaries of your current influence. It may get stuck simply because your position and role in the organization limits your power in other areas. The change will be stuck until you either expand your own influence or find someone to champion the change who has a broader span of influence than you.

Designing ways to avoid these ten common ways change gets stuck is the main work of successful change agents. Inevitably, when your initiative does get stuck, the situation will likely be caused by one of these hazards. Using this workbook, you will work to design ways to avoid getting stuck, and also work through what to do if you find that you are already in a rut. The combination of advance planning and skillful maneuvering as you go will help make your change initiative irresistible.

The Four Drivers of Change

If you read enough books or attend enough training on leadership and change management, you start to realize they all say essentially the same thing. But if everyone knows how to do it, then why does it still feel like pushing a huge boulder uphill? Why does change still get stuck?

Most change management methodologies cover the basics: Leaders need to walk the talk. You need to have a clear vision. Communicate a lot. Set goals. But even the most detailed change management programs are missing a key piece. Unfortunately, leaving it out is what leaves change agents at times wondering why their efforts seem futile.

To illuminate the missing piece, let's look at the four main drivers of changing your organization:

1. Clarify the change
Before you can figure out how to change your organization, you must determine what needs changing. This step involves understanding the current situation and why it needs to change, and determining where the organization should go. Using assessments, surveys, and other analysis, you identify obstacles, challenges and opportunities. Then, clarify what really needs to change to get to the end state. Some of the outputs for this step are the vision, the strategy, desired results, and necessary behaviors.

2. Gain leadership support for change

It is common knowledge that in order for your change initiative to grow beyond your own span of influence you need leadership buy-in. The truth is you need much more than buy-in; as a change agent you need leaders in your organization to take action that supports your initiative. A clear demonstration of management resolve to see the change through to completion breaks through many barriers. Gaining and maintaining the support of leaders is the most essential and challenging role of change agents.

3. Develop structural influence methods

Once you know what needs to change and have the support you need, then you can start to design structural influence methods: the systems, tools and processes that cause and reinforce change. These are the formal programs and tools you install in the organization.

For example, to execute a strategy (Driver 1), you might implement a Balanced Scorecard program (Driver 3). If you want to improve employee performance (1), then you might create a new performance management system (3). If you want to increase productivity (1), you might install new software, or put together a process improvement effort (3). Each of these systems will likely drill down further into new processes, forms, meetings, training, internal communication, incentives and others. All of these examples need leadership support (2).

Typically, these are the things we call change management. If change happened as a result of only leadership support and structural influence methods, then it would be easy! But, there's a piece missing:

4. Leverage personal influence

Personal influence is what sets change in motion. Often, people who implement change stop around Step 3; they figure if they build the system, then everyone else will use it on its own merits. But, the structural influence methods only work if employees and managers use them, and properly at that.

For example, if you are implementing a Balanced Scorecard, it may take some time and effort, but it typically won't take much personal influence to get people to fill out the information on the scorecard. The real challenge begins with getting individuals to use the scorecard to manage and improve their performance.

Skillful change agents will watch out for signs of resistance and even foresee and preempt them. They understand how to gain support and participation from leadership and others. They carefully navigate the potentially awkward, uncomfortable, uncertain moments where meaningful change really happens.

Organizational change happens by keeping leaders on track and installing structural influence methods that are implemented successfully as a result of personal influence. The structural influence methods are the real change that is being managed. If you can get people to use the systems, processes and tools correctly, the change will likely happen. The bulk of your effort as an effective change agent is spent using your personal influence to gain and keep leadership support, and to influence individuals to build and use the systems that will cause the organization to change.

In a nutshell, the missing piece in typical change management methodologies is *you*. This workbook provides the tools to help clarify, organize, and keep track of the things you need to do to successfully influence change in your organization.

The Irresistible Change Model

The model we'll use in this workbook is based on the four drivers of change. Its individual components also help you address and overcome the common ways change gets stuck.

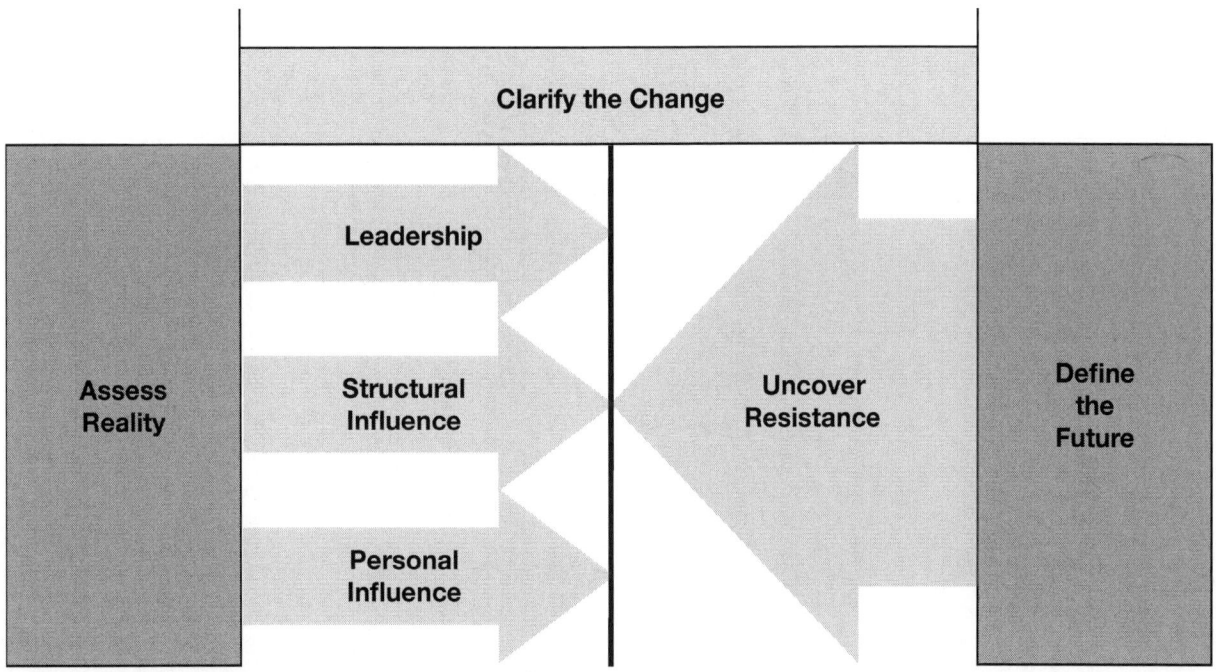

Irresistible Change Model

We start with the first driver, Clarity, which is a set of four components that provide a framework for the remaining drivers. On the left-hand side, we start with Assess Reality to determine the current state of the organization. Next, we Define the Future state on the right-hand side. Once we know where we are now and where we want to be, we then Clarify the Change by analyzing the gap between the two states. As the last step in the Clarify driver, we Uncover Resistance by understanding the obstacles that may prevent forward progress.

If resistance is a force that is pushing us back towards the status quo, then the remaining three drivers are forces that move us towards the future vision. We leverage Leadership to ensure alignment and support of those who have authority within the organization. We build Structural Influence methods to help people move towards the future vision. And we exert our Personal Influence wherever it is needed to engage others and loosen the grip of resistance. Like the Clarity driver, each of these three drivers is broken down into its own components to help you get clear about what to design and how to influence it. These are detailed in the next section.

The model is versatile enough to apply to your entire organization or just to your project or department. You can also use it iteratively to determine what needs to be done at multiple levels. Plus it can be used either at the beginning of a project or anywhere in the middle. I'm certain you will want to come back to it again and again.

How this Workbook is Organized

The *Irresistible Change Guide* is separated into four major areas, based on the four drivers of change. Each area is divided further into specific components of the model.

Clarity

Assess Reality

Before we start to look at the change itself, we start by understanding the organization today. The existing organization gives you the raw materials for change. Assessing the current reality ensures your initiative will not get off to a false start.

Define the Future

Then, we develop a vision of how the organization will work in the future. The vision describes what will have been accomplished once the initiative is complete. It provides both direction and inspiration. When defining the future, we'll stay clear about the goal being the desired result and not just the implementation of the change itself.

Clarify the Change

Next, we assess the gap between current reality and the desired future, to identify the transitions that need to occur. Then we look deeper at each transition to see what really needs to change, to make sure we're not just scratching the surface.

Uncover Resistance

In the last step of gaining clarity about your change initiative, we predict resistance and determine its underlying sources for both the organization and individuals. We also assess inevitable resistance when it occurs. Working to understand the real cause of resistance prevents trying to overcome it with force.

Leadership

Assign Roles and Relationships

First, we figure out your role in the change and the roles of other individuals and groups within the organization. We also define the most effective relationships between the different parties. When everyone has role clarity, fewer things slip through the cracks.

Gain Leadership Support

Next, we determine whose support you need and how much support you need. Then we zero in on how to gain and keep support of specific individuals. Ensuring leaders provide visible, consistent support keeps the organization focused and signals the resolve to make the change happen.

Structural Influence

The Structural Influence section helps you identify the programs, tools and systems to build to help people in your organization make the transition towards the desired future vision. Many of these will be specific to your particular initiative; however, there are two common structural influence methods that are given special attention in this workbook: accountability and communication.

Ensure Accountability

Change is impossible if people don't achieve goals and follow up on their commitments. We start with project goals and measures, and then create accountability agreements for key individuals. Building accountability banishes excuses.

Pinpoint Communication

Haphazard messaging results in scattershot change. Good change communication consists of getting the appropriate message to the right people who then do something with it. In this chapter, we generate a detailed communications plan that hits the target.

Personal Influence

Boost Your Power

Your personal influence relies on building and leveraging your organizational power. We assess your current level and sources of power and then identify ways to boost it. That way, the scope of your initiative is not limited by your own span of influence.

Start Conversations

The most important conversations are usually the ones you would rather avoid. We figure out who you need to talk to most, and then prepare for those conversations. Topics that would otherwise go undiscussed will therefore be addressed instead of undermining progress.

Facilitate Meetings

As a change agent, you will often conduct change in group settings. We explore how to prepare for meetings in advance and, once you get there, how to guide attendees to team effectiveness. Instead of going to meetings to die a slow death, your change initiative will thrive when people get together to work on it.

The Change Management Plan

Key components of this workbook combine to create a comprehensive change management plan. While charts, templates and checklists are interspersed throughout the workbook, these tools are also available as electronic templates so you can print additional copies and complete them together and share with others.

- Status Quo Inventory
- Future State Outlook
- Before And After Chart
- Layers of Change Analysis
- Change Impact Assessment
- Force Field Analysis
- Plan for Resistance Chart
- Roles and Relationships Diagram
- Leadership Support Chart
- Structural Influence Chart
- Initiative Scorecard
- Communication Plan

An index of all templates is listed in the appendix.

READY TO GET STARTED? TURN THE PAGE!

The Scope

You are completing this workbook because you are either setting out to change or are already changing all or part of your organization. I will use the word "organization" through the workbook to refer to the part of the organization you are working to change. So, let's start by identifying what you mean by "organization." Is it the entire organization, a business unit, a department, or a team? Is it a process or program that spans multiple areas? If you put up a fence around the people and processes that will be impacted, who and what would be inside the borders? Setting the scope of your initiative will help you maintain focus throughout the rest of the workbook.

Use the space below to define what you mean by "organization." Use words, or draw a picture.

Define "Organization."

Clarity

Assess Reality

In Praise of the Status Quo

You may find it odd that a guide to implementing change would start by singing the praises of the status quo, a Latin term meaning the current or existing state of affairs. But, the truth is, we change practitioners have given the status quo a bad rap. The status quo is not the enemy to be conquered! Instead, it is the springboard to successful change, if you treat it as such.

When you are responsible for implementing change, it can be tempting to dream about where you want to go and then to start taking immediate steps to move the organization in that direction. But first, it is essential to understand the organization and how it currently works before you start changing it. If you jump out of the blocks before you take a hard look at the status quo, you might soon look back and find that everyone else is still standing back at the starting line.

The status quo, the current way things are done in your organization, provides not only key insights into what should change, but also how to change it. The following are three things you should understand about the organization before you start changing it.

What Not to Change
When things start changing, it can seem like everything is up for grabs. Most likely, there are aspects of the organization that you want to make sure don't get meddled with during the change process. Identifying up front the things you want to keep the same will help maintain stability, and ensure you are not changing things unnecessarily.

What to Leave Behind
When plotting your course on a map, you can't get to where you are going without first knowing where you are now. You need the dot that says, "You are here." Similarly, when planning your project, you need to know what you are changing from, so you can figure out the steps to get to where you want the organization to go. If you start making changes with only the destination in mind, you might find out too late that you started at step 7 instead of step 1.

The Sense of Urgency
As someone who is responsible for the change, you already intuitively know that you are trying to move away from something, even if you haven't articulated it. But, other people will need to see it as well, before they are ready to give up what they are used to. If they are happy and comfortable with the way things are working

now, it might not be enough to have a clear, inspiring vision to get them to try something new. Help people feel dissatisfied with the way things are by communicating a sense of urgency.

It is normal to want to avoid dwelling on the way the organization is now. After all, it's your job to move people away from the status quo! Instead, appreciate the way things are. Develop a fascination for how the status quo is maintained and how it got that way. After all, what you hope to accomplish is making your current change the future status quo.

Next, let's take a look at the elements of an organization that you will assess to see what should stay the same and what should change. Later, we will determine how to create a sense of urgency.

Elements of the Status Quo

Your existing organization is a complex system with many elements that work together (or sometimes don't). You can describe your organization in terms of what you do, why you do it, how you do it, and how well you do it. For each element, you may find strengths and weaknesses. There may be aspects that you want to keep or have more of, and others you want to leave in the past.

Consider the following elements of an organization. After this section, complete the Status Quo Inventory with a description of the current state of your organization for each element. Use the questions below for each element to help guide your descriptions.

What You Do

Products and Services

The organization provides one or more products or services, either for external customers, internal customers, or both. By doing so, it also solves a problem or addresses a need, and adds value in the process. For example, it's been said that people don't need a drill; they need the hole that the drill makes.

- What does your organization do?
- What gaps does it fill with its products and services?

Why You Do It

Mission

An organization's mission is its reason for being. It is the guiding purpose under which people in the organization work together. Most organizations have a mission statement hanging on the lobby wall. Often it is a generic platitude, but when effective, the mission accurately reflects the purpose of the organization and motivates people to come to work every day.

- What is the organization's stated mission, if it has one?
- With what purpose do people come together to work every day?
- How well is the mission aligned with what the organization actually does?

Values

The common values of the people in the organization comprise what is important to the whole. Values guide decisions and priorities. They are reflected in the way people treat each other and deal with customers. They also constrain what the organization spends money on and what behaviors are allowed. The organization's values also guide what it is not willing to do.

- What are your organization's stated values, if it has any?
- What values are reflected in decisions, behaviors and principles?
- How do stated values compare to demonstrated values?

Customers

What you do depends on whom you do it for. Whether internal or external to your organization, your customers include the end consumers of your products and services, plus any intermediaries such as the retailers, wholesalers, or other channels that get the products or services to them. When you have multiple types of customers, they usually have different wants and needs, which are reflected in what you provide each of them. Customers not only provide the organization with revenues or funding. Whom you choose to serve also provides the motivation to do well.

- What types of customers does your organization serve?
- What does each type want, need and expect?
- What is it about your customers that makes your organization want to serve them?

How You Do It

Processes

A process is the step-by-step way work is done. Sometimes processes are defined in formal procedures, and other times they are habits that form undocumented over time. Some processes are standard to most organizations, while others are more unique to the type of work you do.

- Which processes are critical or unique to the operation of the organization?
- How standardized or ad hoc are these processes?

Culture

Often described as "the way we do things around here," culture is the collection of unwritten rules that govern how people behave within the organization. Culture is modeled by leaders and enforced by peer pressure.

- What behaviors of new employees are quickly quashed?
- How would you describe someone who "fits in" with the organization?

Equipment

The equipment we use is the means for getting work done. Equipment consists of the physical equipment we use, such as machinery, tools, supplies, and the environment in which we work. It also includes the technology we use, such as computers, software and digital devices.

- What equipment do employees use to do their jobs?
- What is the physical environment like where the work is done?
- What technology is currently used in the organization?

Policies

Policies are the written rules of the organization. The alignment between policies and culture determine how consistently they are followed and enforced. How consistently they are enforced determines how seriously they are taken.

- Which rules, policies or procedures are strictly enforced?
- Which are largely ignored or inconsistently applied?

Employees

Employees provide talent, the collective skills and knowledge available to get the work done. The alignment between the talent required to do the work and available talent is a factor in determining how well it is done. The strengths, weaknesses, preferences, ambitions and fears of employees impact decisions and inform how things get done. Their personalities shape and are shaped by the culture of the organization.

- What are the predominant talents within the organization?
- What characteristics of employees enable the organization to get its work done?
- What characteristics of employees inhibit the organization?

Structure

The organization is formed by a network of internal and external relationships that work within a formal structure. Some relationships are collegial and others include an element of authority. Some are friendly and others are adversarial. Who works together and how they work together is a strong factor in how work gets done. Relationships are also the avenue of informal communication.

- How do people work together in the organization?
- Who is not "allowed" to work directly with each other?

How Well You Do It

Performance

Performance is how well the organization carries out the work it does. The level of performance can be compared to an objective standard or based on expectations of key stakeholders. Examples are financial performance, customer satisfaction, product quality or process efficiency.

- How well is the organization performing financially compared to expectations?
- How well do the products and services meet the needs and expectations of customers?
- How well does the organization perform its processes?
- What are the current values of measures that demonstrate how well the organization is performing?

Engagement and Morale

Engagement, the level to which employees are active in bringing about the goals of the organization, drives achievement and is a measure of how well the organization works. Engagement is inextricably linked to morale, the collective feelings employees have about their work and the organization. If the status quo of your organization is high morale and high engagement, the case for change may be more difficult to make than if people are dissatisfied and less actively involved in the current state of affairs.

- How active are employees in bringing about success for the organization?
- As a group, how do employees feel about their work and the organization?

Complete the Status Quo Inventory on the next three pages by describing the current status of each element. Use the questions above to help define the status quo. Feel free to expand on this model with existing data, documents, process maps, etc. to create a complete picture of the organization as it works today.

Status Quo Inventory

For each of the elements below, describe your organization as it exists today.

What You Do	
Products & Services	
Why You Do It	
Mission	
Values	
Customers	

Status Quo Inventory

How You Do It	
Processes	
Culture	
Equipment	
Policies	
Employees	
Structure	

Irresistible Change Guide

Status Quo Inventory

How Well You Do It	
Performance	
Engagement & Morale	

In light of these elements, answer the questions on the next two pages to form a clearer picture of the current reality. Start with the things that are good, those you want to keep. Next, list the parts of the status quo you want to leave behind as you embark on this change initiative. Use the Status Quo Inventory as a starting point, but don't feel limited to only use these elements.

What Not to Change

Guided by the following questions, determine what should stay the same during the change. Describe the aspects of the current state that best answer the questions.

What works?

What don't we want to break, mess up, or otherwise meddle with?

What should be protected?

What to Leave Behind

Using the following questions, identify what it is about the current organization that you want to move away from. Describe the aspects of the status quo that best answer the questions.

What could be better?

What needs to be fixed?

What should we stop doing?

A Sense of Urgency

The status quo is comfortable, familiar, and safe. As a result, it begets complacency. In order to break free from the status quo, people need to feel compelled to move away from the way things are and leave it behind. John Kotter described establishing this sense of urgency as the first stage in his foundational book *Leading Change*. Develop a sense of urgency to help people understand that if they keep doing things the same way, something undesirable will happen. Help them realize that the status quo is actually uncomfortable and not a safe place to stay.

The power of urgency comes from the need or desire to stop experiencing the unpleasant. People must feel the discomfort and dissatisfaction with the status quo in order for it to be effective. There is a natural tendency for leaders to put on a happy face and avoid pointing out what isn't working well. But, without the feeling that things aren't so great right now, there will be little energy to move away from the status quo.

What constitutes urgency will depend on the circumstances and values of the organization. Personal loss avoidance is a strong motivator, so the personal consequences of sticking with the current way can invoke a reason to change. At the same time, people also care about other parties other than themselves, so understanding how families, coworkers, community and customers will be impacted by the current trajectory will help generate a sense that "we need to do something about this."

Urgency is not the same as an emergency. It should not crowd out other important activities that keep the organization running. You don't have to drop everything to take care of it, but you're not going to rest while it still needs to be addressed. A smoke alarm going off is an emergency; the regular chirping that tells you it needs a new battery is urgency.

Communicating urgency is not a one-time event. Instead, urgency must be a constant undercurrent of dissatisfaction with the way things are. It is a continual reminder that something different must be done. Any hint that urgency is relenting might signal that it is ok to go back to the way things were.

When you convey a sense of urgency to the organization, you maintain a delicate balance. If the sense of urgency is not strong enough or doesn't strike the right chord, it will be ignored. On the other hand, too much doom and gloom about the current state of affairs can paralyze people or make them think the best option is to jump ship instead of trying to save it.

For the sense of urgency to be effective at energizing change, people must also know what to do to make the discomfort stop. Urgency without a clear direction to get away from the unpleasantness just makes you feel helpless. People must see that the change you make will alleviate the sense of urgency. A proper sense of urgency is best coupled with a clear vision of where they will go once they decide it is worth it to move. In the next chapter, we will explore and create your vision for the future.

For now, answer the questions on the next page to help you clarify your organization's sense of urgency.

Create a Sense of Urgency

Identify why things need to change. Help people feel dissatisfied with the way things are.

Why can't things stay the way they are?

What happens if the organization doesn't change?

How do you want people to feel about the way things are going now?

What is it about the status quo that might generate those feelings?

Define the Future

The Power of a Clear Vision of the Future

The reason for any change is to bring about a better future than would happen if you keep doing the same thing. The next step in gaining clarity for your change initiative is to define that future.

Starting a change initiative without knowing what future you want to bring about is like embarking on a journey without a destination. The result of missing this step can best be summed up by a transaction between Alice and the Cheshire Cat.

> *One day, Alice came to a fork in the road and saw a Cheshire cat in a tree.*
> *"Which road do I take?" she asked. "Where do you want to go?" was his response.*
> *"I don't know," Alice answered. "Then," said the cat, "it doesn't matter."*
> *~Alice's Adventures in Wonderland, Lewis Carroll*

Like Alice, deciding on your organization's future state is a prerequisite to choosing which path you should take to get there. You can't effectively design change unless you are clear about what the end result is. Besides enabling you to chart a course, a clear vision of the future serves four other core purposes, as described below.

Foster Hope

Since your sense of urgency generates a feeling that something is wrong with the way things are now, then the vision of the future provides the antidote. Without an offsetting future to hope for, you are stuck and frustrated in the present with no path forward. The realistic vision of the future offers the hope of eventual improvement that drives you to move forward and gives the organization the energy to take on the challenges and obstacles. Combined with the sense of urgency to get away from the status quo, the vision of a better future compels others to help you get it done.

Inspire the Crowd

While providing hope that the organization can get away from the current state, the future state can also be inspiring in its own right. People want to go there because it is a good place to be. They are energized by the idea of helping bring it to fruition. Being clear about the future allows others to decide they want to go there with you. Achieving the vision becomes a common purpose for the organization to organize itself around.

Share A Common Destination

A clear vision helps others get to the same place even if they go a different route. After all, you can't plan out for every person how they will navigate the change; doing so would not only be impractical, but would also remove any sense of ownership. The vision helps each person figure out his own way of getting there, without having every step prescribed for him. When someone reaches a fork in the road, the vision helps point him toward a decision that will take him closer to the desired future state.

Prepare for What's Next
When you know the weather forecast for tomorrow, it helps you decide what to wear and whether or not to bring an umbrella. In the absence of control, having an idea of what will happen in the future helps you prepare for what it will be like. People with an uncertain future tend to stick with what is safe. When you have a forecast for what will happen, you can prepare people for what is coming before they get there.

With these purposes in mind, let's define the future state that your change initiative will take you to.

Imagine the Future State

The future is wide open and infinite. The possibilities for how it will turn out are virtually endless. At the same time, the future will be the result of a singular path. There is a lot you don't know and can't control, and yet you still need to determine what you want the future to become.

With a stretch of the imagination, let's create what the future will be.

The Timeline

First things first! Before we can start to determine what the organization will look like in the future, we need to determine the timeframe you are aiming for. You want the future state we create to be far enough in the future that there is time for the change to occur, while still being close enough as to be relevant to the organization now.

On the next page, start by setting a marker for how far out in the future we are looking. Then, answer the questions about what the future state looks like.

Where is "There?"

Imagine you are transported to a time after the change initiative has been successfully implemented. Envision yourself as you go about a typical day at the office. Answer the following questions about your organization in its future state.

When have you arrived at the desired future state?

How can you tell that the change was successful?

What seems new or unfamiliar?

What are you and your colleagues proud of having accomplished?

Irresistible Change Guide

Elements of the Future State

In the last chapter, Assess Reality, you described the status quo in terms of each of the fundamental elements of an organization. In this section, we will describe the future state for each of the same elements. Take a moment to review your Status Quo Inventory, the description of the current state.

For some elements, you may want to keep aspects the same as in the Status Quo Inventory. For the elements that you said you want to leave behind, you will list how things will be different in the future.

Consider again the following elements of an organization. After this section, complete the Future State Outlook with a description of the imagined future state for each element. Describe your organization in terms of what you will do, why you will do it, how you will do it, and how well you will do it. Use the questions below for each element to help guide your descriptions.

What You Will Do

Products and Services
- What will your organization do?
- What products or services will it provide?
- What needs will it fill with its products and services?

Why You Will Do It

Mission
- What will the organization's stated mission be?
- With what purpose will people come together to work every day?

Values
- What will your organization's stated values be?
- How will decisions, behaviors and principles be different based on those values?

Customers
- What types of customers will your organization serve?
- What will each type want, need and expect?
- Which types of customers will your organization stop serving?
- What is it about your customers that will make you want to serve them?

How You Will Do It

Processes
- Which processes will be critical or unique to the operation of the organization?
- What processes will have been introduced?
- How standardized or ad hoc will these processes be?

Culture
- What behaviors of new employees will be allowed by their peers?

- How do you describe someone who will "fit in" with the organization?
- How will culture work to keep the organization in its future state?

Equipment
- What equipment will employees use to do their jobs?
- What will the physical environment like where the work will be done?
- What technology will be used in the organization in the future state?

Policies
- What rules, policies or procedures will be created?
- Which will now be strictly enforced?
- Which will be eliminated?

Employees
- What talents will be prominent in the organization?
- What characteristics of employees will enable the organization to get its work done?
- What characteristics of employees will be diminished?

Structure
- How will people be organized to work together?
- Which relationships will be improved?

How Well You Will Do It

Performance
- How well will the organization perform financially?
- How well will the products and services meet the needs and expectations of customers?
- How well will the organization perform its processes?
- What are the future values of measures that demonstrate how well the organization will perform?

Engagement and Morale
- How active will employees be in bringing about success for the organization?
- As a group, how will employees feel about their work and the organization?

Complete the Future State Outlook on the next three pages with descriptions for each element. Remember to keep the same time line as you defined earlier in the chapter.

Future State Outlook

Describe your organization as you imagine it will be once the change initiative is implemented.

What You Will Do	
Products & Services	
Why You Will Do It	
Mission	
Values	
Customers	

Future State Outlook

How You Will Do It	
Processes	
Culture	
Equipment	
Policies	
Employees	
Structure	

Irresistible Change Guide © 2014 Enclaria LLC

Future State Outlook

How Well You Will Do It	
Performance	
Engagement & Morale	

Vision Statement

Now that you have created a clear picture of what the future should look like, let's boil it down to a vision statement that is easy to communicate and remember.

Every change initiative needs a clear, well-articulated vision of the desired state, whether it is a specific outcome goal ("We will be #1 provider of widgets in 5 years.") or an organizational goal ("By 201X we will have the best team in the industry.") The description of the future target defines the scope of the transformation and sets the timetable.

Besides being a clear picture of the future, a good vision statement has the following three traits:

- It is inspiring. People want to go there.
- It is compelling. People need to go there to get away from the status quo.
- It is realistic. People believe they can go there.

Using the information you developed in this chapter, create some possible vision statements that describe the destination for your change initiative. Select one that resonates with those who will share the same future.

Vision statement: We will...

Clarify the Change

Now that we have two pictures of the organization, one as it is and one you would like to create, we can start to focus on the transformation between the two. First, we will describe the before-and-after state of the organization. Next, we will dive deeper into each of the pieces that are changing as we look at multiple layers of change and the expected impact on the organization. Then, we will start to map out the factors that will help or hinder the change.

Organizational change is not a linear process, and neither is designing it. The exercises in this chapter will help you look at your change initiative in different ways so you can create a clear picture of what you are trying to do. Although they build on each other, you might find as you go through these next exercises that you discover something in one that informs one you already completed. If that happens, update the previous chart so you have a complete description of the change.

Before and After

Now that you have an idea of what needs to change, let's clarify the change even further by forming a complete before-and-after picture of the organization. You likely have all the components already figured out; it is just a matter of organizing them in the chart that follows.

In the previous chapters, we assessed the current organization and defined the future around common elements of an organization. In this chapter, we will narrow the change down into key transition themes. You can think of Transition Themes as what's changing. The Transition Themes for your initiative may be more specific than the elements we described in the Status Quo Inventory and Future State Outlook, or they may cross multiple elements. In a nutshell, you want to describe what is changing in your own language that makes sense for your organization.

First, boil down the key concepts of what is changing into short, meaningful phrases that describe the parts of the organization that will change as part of this initiative. These are your Transition Themes, which you will list in the middle column of the Before and After Chart.

Next, in the From column, describe the current state of the Transition Theme in that row. This column describes that part of the organization as it is now.

Then, in the To column, describe the future vision for the Transition Theme in that row. This column shows how the organization will be different when the initiative is complete. To underscore the elements of the organization that you want to protect throughout the change, include them in the Before and After Chart, but keep the same description both before and after to show that they are not changing.

Consider the fictitious example of ABC Corp, an organization that historically has built predictable products with existing technology. ABC Corp has a vision to become a more innovative company. It wants to develop and sell innovative products, and knows that to do so requires not just new technology, but a shift to a more nimble workforce.

Using the example from ABC Corp, what you want is something that communicates the changes like this:

From	Transition Theme	To
Predictable products with existing technology	Products	Innovative products
Maximize asset utilization	Technology	Strategic investments in new technology
Staid	Workforce	Nimble

Example Before and After Chart for ABC Corp

After you fill in the following Before and After Chart for your organization, compare it to the organization as you described it in the first two chapters. What themes appeared in either the current state assessment or the future state vision, but do not appear here? Decide whether they should be included and if so, add them to the Before and After Chart.

Before and After Chart

From	Transition Theme	To

Irresistible Change Guide

The Four Layers of Change

One of the difficult parts of implementing organizational change is that what really needs to change is not as it appears on the surface. What you initially think you are changing is usually only a part of the complete picture. There are multiple layers underneath — aspects of the organization and the people who make it up — that will also need to change in order to achieve the change at the surface.

The following are the four layers of change. For each Transition Theme you identified in the last section, we will peel it back and reveal where you should focus your own efforts:

Outcome

At the surface of the change is the outcome. It is the reason you are changing anything at all; you want to cause a different result than what the organization has achieved in the past. Whether the outcome is earnings, customer service, efficiency, effectiveness, or morale, any organizational change has a needle it is expected to move.

For ABC Corp, to achieve the vision of becoming a more innovative company, the desired outcome of the change initiative is to add more innovative products to its portfolio.

A change in outcome, of course, does not occur magically on its own. You have to dig deeper to determine how to cause the needle to move.

Process

Peel off the surface layer, and you will expose a change in process. In order to achieve the outcome, you will most likely need to create, improve, or dismantle at least one process. The process might be a step-by-step flow of activities, or it might be a set of cause-and-effect assumptions for how to achieve the outcome. Either way, you are changing how work gets done in the organization.

For ABC Corp, the initiative will focus mainly on the new product development process, especially the idea generation phase. New activities will be added to improve creativity. The current steps for vetting ideas will gain new criteria for selecting ideas that will be developed.

Behavior

To implement a process effectively, individuals must change their own behaviors. Some might have a new task to perform. Others may need to act differently in meetings or in relationships. Some may have a new form or report to complete. And, some may need to communicate differently. Determine the behaviors that individuals need to add, change, or stop in order to support the change.

At ABC Corp, the key behaviors identified are for marketing to solicit ideas from new sources, and to use the new criteria for vetting ideas. In meetings where new product ideas are discussed, people are now expected to defer judgment and explore all ideas.

Mindset

Underlying the behaviors of individuals is the collective set of conditions that either encourage or discourage people from doing them. There are a number of factors that motivate behaviors in this layer, such as attitudes, perceptions, habits, beliefs, emotions and organizational culture.

The main factor affecting performance of new behaviors at ABC Corp is the attitude toward risk-taking. At an individual level, employees need to become comfortable sharing wild ideas. Managers need to believe it is worthwhile to break from past successes and pursue uncharted territory.

Now, we will work through the layers to determine the underlying factors that will ultimately cause your desired result. Although change becomes more difficult with each layer that you expose, the deeper you go, the more sustainable the result.

For each Transition Theme on the Before and After Chart, complete the Layers of Change Analysis on the next page. First, copy one transition at a time to the section at the top of the page (one transition per page). Determine whether the transition you listed is an outcome, process, behavior or mindset change and add it to the corresponding row. Complete the rest of the Layers of Change Analysis by detailing the remaining layers. Then, at the bottom, list the groups or individuals who are involved in implementing this transition theme and those who are affected by the transition theme.

Starting at the top and working your way down, answer the following questions in the spaces provided:

1. What **outcomes** will change?

2. What **process** changes will lead to the new outcomes?

3. What **behavior** changes will create the process and outcome changes? Whose behaviors need to change?

4. What **mindset** changes will encourage the behavior changes?

Using ABC Corp as an example, the Transition Theme of Products would break down like this:

Layer	From	To
Outcome	Predictable products with existing technology	Innovative products
Process	A new product process that limits what items we consider viable	A new product process that encourages and enables innovations
Behavior	Stick with items we know will work	Actively solicit creative ideas from new sources
Mindset	Failure is bad	Failure is an opportunity to learn and improve

By completing the Layers of Change Analysis, you will have a list of the key elements of your organization that you plan to change, along with a cause and effect analysis.

Irresistible Change Guide

Layers of Change Analysis

From	Transition Theme	To

Layer	From		To
Outcome			
Process			
Behavior			
Mindset			

Who is involved?	Who else is affected?

The Effect on Stakeholders

By definition, a stakeholder is anyone who has something at stake due to your change. A stakeholder is not just the person who must change the way they work in order to gain the desired results. A stakeholder may also be someone who benefits or suffers from the outcome of the change, or someone who must support the change in order for it to happen. "Stakeholder" is the generic term for anyone who is impacted by or who impacts the change.

When you're designing your change initiative, you'll modify your approach to different stakeholders based on features that are unique to each. Since you probably don't have the capacity to deal with every person individually, first determine the different groups of stakeholders. You may divide the organization into groups based on:

Organization Level
Split the organization by title: executives, upper-management, middle-management, supervisors, front-line employees.

Departments, Functional Areas or Business Units
Group people by the task they have in relation to your initiative, or by natural organizational boundaries.

Regional or Geography
Divide the organization by regions or languages.

Union or Non-Union
Split employees between those in a bargaining unit and those that are not.

External Stakeholders
Consider groups that are not a part of the organization, such as the media, the public, regulators and the community.

On the next page, list the stakeholder groups for your change initiative. Use terminology that is familiar to your organization. In the next section, we'll take a closer look at each group with the Change Impact Assessment.

Stakeholder List

	Stakeholder Group
a	
b	
c	
d	
e	
f	
g	

To influence change, there are several things you should know about the stakeholders in your organization to help tailor your approach. These features will help you further slice and dice your organization so you can best target communication, training, and other instruments of change.

Characteristics

Once you identify your stakeholder groups, identify some of the characteristics that make each group unique. Who are they and what do they do? Learn things like what role they play in the organization, how they work together, and what values they uphold.

Transitions

Before you can understand the impact the change will have on each stakeholder group, you must know the transitions the group will undergo. What's really changing? Part of the change is probably external – a change to the environment, structure, or process – and part is internal – behaviors, attitudes, beliefs, or values.

Impact ON Change

You not only want to understand how each stakeholder group is impacted by the change, but also what their impact on the change is. What are the essential responsibilities they have regarding the change? What happens if they don't participate? Identify stakeholders' roles in the change and how they can best contribute.

Impact BY Change

Next, anticipate how the stakeholders will be impacted by the change. Understand how people will be affected as transitions happen around them and within them. Remember the impact may be both positive and negative, and it is important to recognize both. What will they like or dislike about the change? What emotions will likely be triggered by the change? Since they are stakeholders, what is really at stake for them?

Supporting Factors

For each group, identify what it is about the group that will help move change forward. Some supporting factors may be teamwork or culture. Perhaps they already have the necessary expertise or attitudes. Recognize the assets each group already has on hand that support the change, so you can build from there.

Obstructing Factors

Lastly, you want to know what aspects of the group help maintain the status quo. What are the unspoken rules for working together that keep things the way they are? Understand the nature of the glue – culture, behaviors, history, or other traits – that may keep the group from moving forward. Later on, we'll identify further the potential sources of resistance that may crop up within that group as the change unfolds.

Change is not a one size fits all endeavor. It is essential to tailor your approach to the people who will experience and implement it. Learning what you can about the people who impact and are impacted by the change will go a long way towards designing an initiative that will achieve the desired results.

For each stakeholder group you identified, complete the Change Impact Assessment on the next page.

Change Impact Assessment

Stakeholder Group:

Characteristics

Transitions		
From	**Transition Theme**	**To**

Impact ON Change	Impact BY Change

Supporting Factors	Obstructing Factors

Closing the Gap

The ultimate objective of your change initiative is to close the gap between the status quo and the future vision.

To visualize the factors that will help or hinder you in your quest for change, we will use Force-Field Analysis, a tool developed by Kurt Lewin, one of the pioneers of social psychology and organization development.

In the following diagram, imagine the line down the center of the chart can slide horizontally left and right. When the line moves to the right, that means the change is successfully moving toward the Future Vision. If the line moves to the left, then the organization is stuck in the Status Quo. The forces on the left side are pushing against the line to the right, in the direction of progress toward change. The forces on the right-hand side push against it to the left, working against the change.

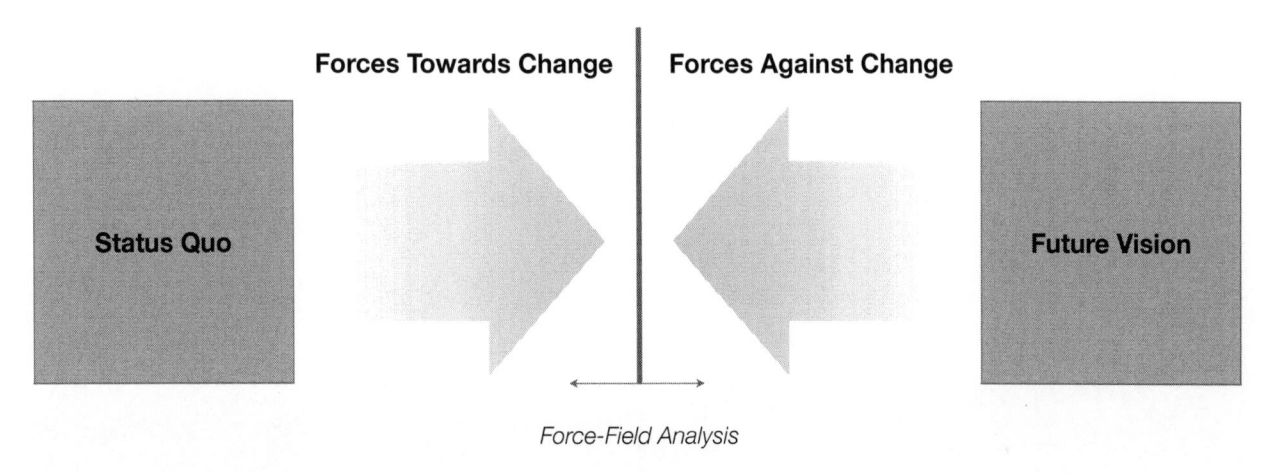

Force-Field Analysis

Once you identify the existing and expected factors that will affect your ability to implement change, you can design ways to make the forces towards change stack up in your favor. In the rest of this workbook, we will approach the change design in the following ways:

- Strengthen the existing factors that support change
- Weaken those forces that work against change
- Design new factors that will create the desired change.

Let's take stock of the factors we've identified so far. Complete the Force Field Analysis on the next page for each Transition Theme for which you filled out the Layers of Change Analysis.

Start by looking at what aspects of the current or future states already support your change initiative. Considering all four layers of change, list the existing forces that support or enable change in the left-hand Forces Towards Change column. Review the work you have done so far, this time with an eye for what you can leverage to maintain or gain energy for change.

Next, summarize those elements you've identified so far that may hinder the change. List the obstructing factors you identified in the Change Impact Assessment in the right-hand Forces Against Change column. We'll dig further into resistant forces in the next chapter.

Irresistible Change Guide

Force Field Analysis

From	Transition Theme	To

Forces Towards Change	Forces Against Change

In the rest of this workbook, we will design the remaining three drivers of change. We will use them to strengthen supporting organizational factors, weaken resistant factors, and add new ways to influence change. If we were to add the three drivers to your Force-Field Analysis, it would look something like this:

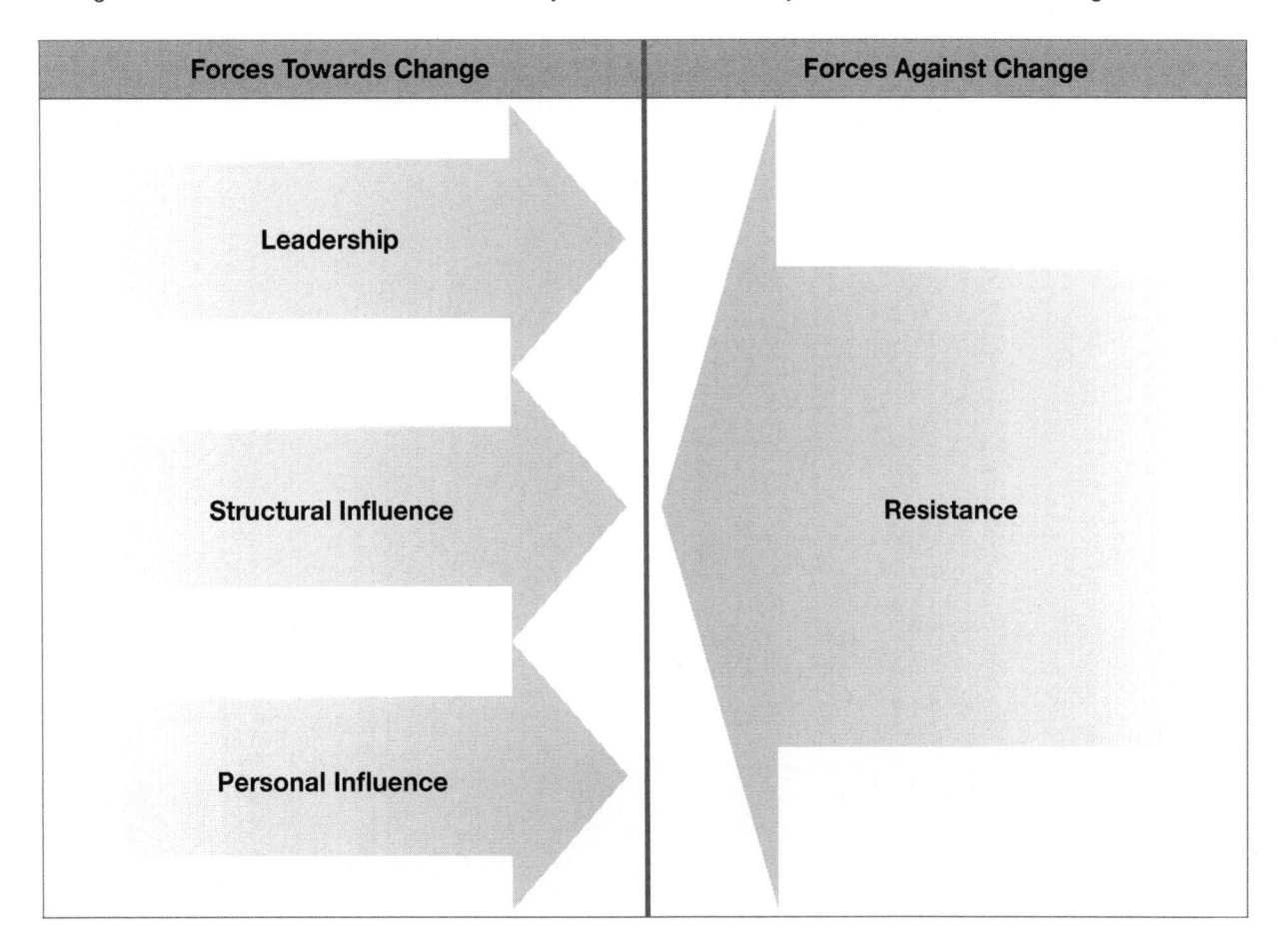

Forces Towards Change	Forces Against Change
Leadership	Resistance
Structural Influence	
Personal Influence	

Before we can start designing the factors that will drive change, we need to understand the resistance you might face or are facing as you implement your change initiative.

Uncover Resistance

Behind the Mask of Resistance

Anyone who has implemented change in an organization has encountered it: the feeling that you are dragging a heavy weight, or pushing a boulder uphill, swimming upstream, or banging your head against the wall. The label we put on the sense of being slowed down or stuck is *resistance*.

Taking the resistance label at face value causes us to blame others for not immediately changing, and gives the impression that there are people in the organization who are either rising up or using subversive methods to stop the change initiative. If we treat resistance as something to be overcome by pushing harder, we end up getting more resistance in return. It is a dangerous mindset for a change agent to believe that the people in the organization are essentially the enemy, needing to be vanquished.

The truth is resistance is not something to be overcome, but something to be uncovered. Resistance is in the eye of the beholder. In fact, what change agents experience as resistance when someone else does it seems rational and justified when we do it ourselves. I have heard it jokingly said that resistance means "you are not doing what I want you to do with the speed or enthusiasm I expect."

The following behaviors are commonly interpreted as resistance, and are really symptoms of underlying factors.

Push Back

As a change agent, when someone speaks up against the change, giving reasons why it won't work, it is easy to get defensive. If you brush it off as excuses that can be ignored, you are missing a great opportunity to gain buy-in. First of all, his warning might be a valid point that you had not considered, so it would be wise to pay attention. And, the more you listen to, understand, and address concerns, the more he will feel like a participant in the change instead of someone to be bowled over.

Procrastination

Someone keeps putting off tasks that you think he should have completed yesterday. When people seem to do everything else first before working on the change, it may be that their priorities are out of whack, or simply different from yours. They believe they will be most successful by focusing on other things. Or, it could be that they are avoiding the change out of fear, lack of skills, or confusion.

Malicious Compliance

Sometimes people say they agree with the change and go through the motions. They do exactly what is asked — to a fault. It seems they remove themselves from accountability by precisely following instructions, even if a better outcome would come from using their own ingenuity. The term "malicious compliance," like resistance, indicates a sinister intent; however, it could be that the bare minimum is all they have time for, or that fear is preventing them from coloring outside the lines.

Laying Low

Others during change keep their head down, seeming to not want to get involved. They might think they can outlast the change initiative if they just pretend it is not happening. Based on past experience or the messages they are getting from leadership, they believe that if they wait long enough, the change will just go away. Understanding why they are hiding in plain sight can reveal gaps in your implementation that are leaving people skeptical about leadership resolve.

Going Rogue

Sometimes a person, group or department will take the change and run with it — in a direction you may not have intended. Or they might tweak the process or the message in a way that diminishes alignment and consistency with the rest of the organization. To you it seems like they are not going with the program. But to the people going through the change, it feels like ownership. They are putting their own stamp on it to make it fit, and to feel a sense of control.

Resistance is what you feel as a change agent after telling yourself a story to interpret others' behaviors that seem to be working against the change. There is always an alternate story behind the mask of resistance that explains their behavior. Only once you understand the root of resistance can you design effective means of influencing change.

Answer the questions on the next page to identify the current symptoms of resistance in your organization. Then, we will start to uncover the underlying sources of that resistance.

Symptoms of Resistance

In what ways are people causing you frustration?

Who seems to be resisting change? What are they doing that makes you say that?

What symptoms of resistance do you notice? By whom?

What resistance techniques do people in your organization use successfully to avoid change?

There are two types of resistance you must deal with when implementing organizational change: personal resistance and organizational resistance. All resistance is inherently personal; each individual chooses to participate in the change or not. However, the organization as a system has ways to keep things the same, which I call organizational resistance.

First, let's look at the sources of personal resistance.

Eight Sources of Personal Resistance

Organizational change is not an immediate phenomenon. Thankfully so – if things changed as quickly as we wished they would, we would all have whiplash!

The fact is, we cannot change the attitudes and habits of others. We can only do our best to influence them, alleviate the things that cause resistance, and wait to see if it works. Each person processes change through the lens of his own experiences, preferences, personality, and emotions. And that happens in other people's timing, not necessarily in yours. Before we start talking about the reasons people may not change as fast as you want, let's acknowledge that it may just be that they need more time to go through the process of changing themselves.

That said, the role of the change agent is to help people change, so in this section, we will take a look at the reasons people don't.

Resistance does not exist in the absence of your own expectations. In other words, you perceive someone else's resistance to change when you have an expectation that he should be doing something different than he is actually doing. Is that person really resisting the change, or is there something else missing?

Let's take a look at the only source of resistance on this list that is an objection to the change itself.

Valid Concerns

One of the assumptions going into this workbook is that the change you are trying to implement is in fact something you should be doing — one that brings about improvement, helps people work better, and makes the organization more successful. However, not all change is good, and perhaps yours is flawed in some way. If so, someone in your organization has probably already figured it out and is trying to tell you, so listen closely to objections.

There is always a valid reason for resistance. Many times concerns are personal and natural, and can be addressed without impact to the initiative. Other times, people follow a logical path to the conclusion that the change is not going to work, or will have negative side effects. Don't brush off objections as resistance that you can ignore and keep pushing forward! Instead, seek to understand the objections, and ask yourself: What is the likelihood that the change will follow this path? What happens if it does? If there is a chance that the initiative is the wrong move, you can start small to test it out or otherwise mitigate risk before going full-bore. Plus, your initiative will be more robust, and you will have more buy-in from people whom you respect enough to understand and address their resistance.

When the project is already in process, there is a fine line between the symptoms of a bad idea and poor implementation. If you are seeing unintended and unexpected consequences occurring during the implementation, determine whether the consequences are an artifact of the change process (e.g. poor communication or lack of leadership support) or of the change itself (e.g. the new process didn't save as much as you expected, or customers didn't like the change as much as you thought they would). If there is a problem with the change process, then you can work to get it back on track. If the problem is the change itself, no amount of change management is going to solve the problem.

Let's take a look at the remaining seven sources of resistance, which are all artifacts of the change process. By helping people eliminate these sources, you will smooth the path towards implementation.

Information

One source of resistance is a lack of information. Without enough information about the change, uncertainty abounds. In the absence of information, people tend to fill the void with the worst case scenario. Many would rather stay where they are than risk stepping out in the wrong direction.

Since resistance is a product of your own expectations, if the other person does not know what your expectations are, then it will be difficult for him to meet them. Likewise, someone who does not have the same information as you, or the same understanding of it as you, might come to a different conclusion and choose to act differently than you would expect. Besides just receiving the information, the other person also must understand it, believe it and internalize it.

The types of missing information that might cause resistance are numerous. Some may not have seen a viewpoint that would lead to a sense of urgency. Perhaps the vision has not been communicated, or is unclear. There are a number of details about the change that may have gone un-communicated, unreceived, or misunderstood.

To discover an information gap, ask the question, "What might he not know or understand?" Identify where the communication breakdown is happening.

Skills

Resistance may be the result of a skill deficit. In order to change, people must be capable of doing so. When they feel they are unable to change, resistance ensues.

When someone doesn't know how to do something, or doesn't feel confident in his ability, he might feel embarrassed to try. He may not tell you he doesn't know how, but may procrastinate or exhibit another symptom of resistance instead.

The person may need additional knowledge or training in order to know how to complete the expected activities or behaviors. The change initiative might require new technological skills. Managers may lack leadership skills such as holding people accountable or communication skills.

To discover a skill gap, ask, "What might he be unable to do?" A clear understanding of the skills involved in implementing the change, plus an assessment to determine the skills that exist in the organization, may help you find which individuals need training or additional knowledge transfer.

Motivation

Resistance is often attributed to a lack of motivation, which explains why, in some organizations, incentive programs are the default tool to entice people to participate in change. Without trying to understand the underlying motives that would drive change, we resort to a motivation proxy; we assume that people won't want to do what is expected, so we offer something of value in exchange. Change incentives can be an expensive endeavor and often end up with unintended consequences, including diminishing the intrinsic value of the change itself.

Motivation is a matter of choice that shows up in priorities and reflects values. Those that lack the motivation to participate in the change or to take on new behaviors are choosing to do something else instead. Either they don't see the value in participating in the change, or something else is taking precedence over the initiative. The project or the necessary behaviors may not be aligned with what they consider to be important. If a change is going to make someone's job more difficult or negatively impact him, expect him to be unmotivated and unhappy with the change.

To discover a motivation gap, ask, "What does he prioritize ahead of the change initiative?" How someone spends his limited resources is a good indicator of his values. Then, you can identify how the change initiative matches up with his existing priorities.

Power

People often resist change when they feel powerless to implement it. They may have the personal ability and the desire to participate, but they believe they are not in a position to do so.

Sometimes this lack of power is real. The boss or someone else with authority knowingly contradicts the change message and specifically directs his subordinates not to participate. Not many people would deliberately violate the boss's orders in that situation. They may not speak up about it either, and will compensate with resistant behaviors.

Often the lack of power is perceived, based on the interpretation of behaviors of someone with authority. Misalignment between the change message and the behaviors, decisions, and words of authority figures is translated as not fully agreeing with the change. Bosses who do not model the desired behaviors themselves send the message that they are not bought in. Bosses that second guess or judge their employees in the midst of change inadvertently punish people for participating, even if they really want the change to happen. When that occurs, people will not feel empowered to change, and the change will stall.

To discover a power gap, ask, "Who really has control?" Human beings crave the perception that they are in control. When they feel that they aren't, they will demonstrate resistance.

Fear

Fear is at the root of much of resistance. Change by definition means taking a risk by doing something different from what probably has brought success in the past. Fear is the expectation that if you take the risk, then something bad might happen. When fear results in the avoidance of that risk, you will see resistance.

Asking someone to perform new activities and behaviors may conjure up many types of fear. At work, people may be afraid of:

Failure	Looking stupid	Being wrong
Rejection	Not being good enough	Losing power
Losing popularity	Inferiority	Retribution
Damaging relationships	Letting people in	Being challenged

To discover a fear gap, ask, "What is he avoiding?" Fears may be individual, a result of preferences and past experiences. Some fears are universal but experienced to varying degrees. Threats to our wellbeing, sense of control, status, and autonomy are some. Uncertainty and being shunned by the group are also fears that everyone experiences. Anticipating how your change will trigger fear will provide clues for how to negate it.

Trust
Sometimes people resist the messenger of change. In any other circumstance, they would participate, but they hold back because they don't like or don't trust one or more people who advocate for it. The relationship with the untrusted person affects the perception of the project.

Trust is a foundation of change. Stepping into an uncertain future is an act of faith, which requires trust that those who are setting the direction are choosing the right path. People must believe they will be supported and that their efforts will not be futile.

There are many places where trust can break down. A lack of trust may stem from a history of faltered change initiatives. People may not believe the change will succeed because they doubt the credibility or resolve of the leader or leaders who are driving the change. People who don't get along may not want to support each other during the change.

To discover a trust gap, ask, "Who or what might he doubt?" It may be easy to see where others are losing trust, but remember, this one might require a look in the mirror.

Resources
If any source of resistance is going to be verbalized, it is a lack of resources. Not having enough time or money can be a valid excuse for why progress is not being made. Resource constraints factor into decisions about which activities will be completed and supported, and which will be ignored or postponed.

Lack of resources is also an easy excuse, and may be a symptom of another source of resistance. When someone complains of a resource constraint, it could be that he is prioritizing another activity ahead of the change initiative, which would be a motivation gap. He may fear delegation or attempting the change. Or, if he is inefficient at the task, there may be a skill gap.

To discover a resource gap, ask, "What may be his constraint?" Identify the limiting factor. Then, just to check, ask yourself, "What other source of resistance may be in play?"

You can plan ahead to diminish the resistance you expect will happen, but you will never eliminate all of it. People are just too unpredictable to create a perfect plan in advance. You will also have to deal with the resistance you encounter along the way.

We will work to uncover personal resistance from two different angles. Using the Plan for Resistance template on the next page, we will plan ahead for the resistance you might expect during your change initiative, so you can design the change to mitigate it in advance. With the Individual Resistance Assessment template, you can analyze what might be behind the resistance exhibited by a specific person, so you can handle it on a case-by-case basis as it happens.

Plan for Resistance

In the last chapter you identified the gap between the current state and the future vision, and analyzed four layers of change to determine the processes, behaviors and motivation changes that need to occur in order to achieve the desired outcome. You also assessed the impact the change will have on different stakeholder groups. Continuing to build your Force Field Analysis, we will now determine what forces against change fit in the right hand side of the chart.

For each transition theme you identified, review your Layers of Change Analysis, and for each stakeholder group, review the Change Impact Assessment. The Layers of Change Analysis details your high-level expectations for the organization: what you want to stop doing, what you want to start doing, and, for those items that stay the same, what you want to continue doing. The Change Impact Assessment identifies what each stakeholder group will go through as the change is implemented. Now, we will take a look at the resistance you might encounter that would prevent the organization from making the transition.

Complete the Plan for Resistance Chart on the next page for each transition theme and stakeholder group. At the top, identify the stakeholder group and select and enter information about the transition theme. Next, identify the sources of resistance that are currently maintaining the gap between the status quo and the future vision. Going through each of the eight sources of personal resistance, brainstorm the resistance you might expect as the organization moves through the transition. What sources of resistance might prevent you from achieving the future vision, and how?

Plan for Resistance Chart

Stakeholder Group:

From	Transition Theme	To
	→	

Source	Expected Resistance
Valid Concerns	
Information	
Skills	
Motivation	
Power	
Fear	
Trust	
Resources	

Irresistible Change Guide

Assess Individual Resistance

While the potential sources you just identified will help to anticipate and reduce resistance, you can never predict and plan for all the ways people might react to the change. During the course of implementing change, you will encounter people that seem like they are resisting change. As a change agent, it is your responsibility to determine the underlying causes of this resistance and then to find ways to influence those individuals and help them move beyond it. Use the assessment on the next page whenever you encounter resistance from someone, to determine what might be driving that behavior. As we continue with the workbook, you can then figure out what to do about it.

Identify the person who demonstrates resistance at the top of the page.

Next, identify the expectations you have that are not being met.

- What would you like him to start doing differently?
- What would you like him to stop doing?

Then, list the overt behaviors or actions by that person that you have determined are symptoms of resistance. Some examples we discussed earlier were:

- Push back
- Procrastination
- Malicious compliance
- Laying low
- Going rogue

Last, specify the potential sources of resistance the individual may be experiencing. In each of the boxes provided, explore how that source may be causing the person to demonstrate the symptoms or not meet expectations.

Please note, this is a tool for your personal use. It may not be wise to share this assessment directly with the individual in question. However, it will help you see the change initiative from his point of view and explore what might be causing him to demonstrate resistance.

Individual Resistance Assessment

Name:

Expectations

Symptoms

Potential Sources of Personal Resistance	
Valid Concerns	Power
Information	Fear
Skills	Trust
Motivation	Resources

Break the Bonds of Organizational Resistance

The status quo, the current way things are done in your organization, came about because it was successful. People in your organization learned how to conduct their jobs through trial and error. The things that worked were incorporated into how things are done, and the things that didn't work were dropped. Over time, these became habits that are reinforced by daily interactions with other people in the organization. Unfortunately, these learned patterns now stand in the way of your change initiative and create organizational resistance.

Even though circumstances have changed and the current way is undesirable to the organization, the status quo sticks because it still brings about success for individuals. Success to individuals is more than the overt achievement of goals. Rather, success is marked by the favorable outcomes of our day-to-day work. The reinforcement of the status quo is subtle and often occurs invisibly. Consider the following factors that secretly define success.

Progress

People stick with what works. Over time, we learn the processes, behaviors, and interactions that get the job done. Since these were successful in making progress in the past, we assume they will continue to work in the future.

When you are implementing change, past progress can be a blind spot to the new circumstances. If people are able to achieve their personal goals without participating in the change, you have misalignment. If they are getting results, even while doing unwanted activities, then the status quo will continue to have a strong hold.

Rewards

We tend to think of rewards as incentives, raises, promotions and recognition, as these are powerful guide rails that maintain the status quo if not aligned with the change. However, perceived rewards go beyond official programs. Positive reactions such as agreement, acceptance, a bump in status, or an increase in autonomy make us want to repeat the performance. In the absence of feedback, getting away with an undesirable behavior means it's okay to do it next time.

The positive feedback — or the lack of negative feedback — people perceive when they continue their same old behaviors gets in the way of change. When they are told to do one thing but are inadvertently rewarded for doing another, the mixed messages mean one thing: stick with what works.

Safety

At our core, people crave security, consistency, and control. Given a choice, we tend to prefer low risk. We stay away from making mistakes. We avoid uncertainty. Getting through the day without a fear being realized ticks a mark in the success column.

Unfortunately, change is not inherently safe. It is chock full of uncertainty, because it involves doing something new, which might not work immediately or turn out the way we planned. Without giving themselves the latitude to take risks and make mistakes, people remain where they are, doing what is familiar and proven instead.

Harmony

As social creatures, we want to be liked by others. For the good of the group, we want everyone to get along. As a result, we maintain harmony and avoid conflict. Fitting in with the team is success; being shunned or ridiculed is not.

During change, we need conflict. Open conversations about concerns expose personal resistance so it can be understood and dealt with. Accountability is nonexistent when people are protecting harmony instead of asking difficult questions. Maintaining harmony results in lack of constructive disagreement and withholding of ideas. Nodding heads agree with change, but they don't necessarily implement it.

If your organization seems stuck in the status quo, chances are that people are still experiencing success by doing things the same old way. Find the perceived successes that maintain the status quo, so you can decrease the personal benefits of maintaining the status quo and create new perceptions of success that enable change.

Answer the questions on the next page to help uncover the forces at work on individuals by the organization.

Organizational Resistance Exercise

How does desired behavior get discouraged?

In what ways are undesirable behaviors still successful?

What are the subtle ways the status quo is reinforced?

How does "the way the organization works" enhance personal resistance of those within it?

Move Beyond Resistance

The rest of this workbook is dedicated to helping you design ways to move beyond the resistance you uncovered in this chapter to achieve the future vision.

Having gained clarity about the sources of resistance, you probably already have a number of ideas for how to work through it. The following are some guidelines for how to reduce resistance for each of the sources. I have also included which sections of this workbook might help you best.

Valid Concerns

When people have concerns that the change itself is ill-advised, the best thing you can do is listen and address those concerns. Invite them to participate to help make the outcome better. If possible, pilot the change on a small scale to test and improve it.

- *See: Start Conversations*

Information

Decrease resistance by providing clarity. Provide direction and convey a sense of urgency to move away from the status quo. Gather additional information if necessary to provide evidence that your change will be effective. Make sure that each person knows what is expected or required. Consider different methods of communication to share your message.

- *See: Pinpoint Communication*

Skills

Where you identify a skills gap, work first to acknowledge the gap. Design training or provide other learning opportunities to boost the skills required to successfully implement the change.

- *See: Structural Influence*

Motivation

Armed with information and skills, the person needs the motivation to act accordingly. Motivation is either intrinsic (internally-based), such as wanting to do a good job or a good deed, or extrinsic (externally-based), like earning a reward or prize. Align the change initiative with values and interests to motivate people to participate.

- *See: Structural Influence; Ensure Accountability*

Power

People must have the power to act in ways that enable the change. A gap occurs when an essential leader is not expressing or lending needed support. Map power gaps to the source and work to get the right leaders to support the change by empowering their people.

- *See: Gain Leadership Support*

Fear

Where fear is discovered, try to neutralize it by reducing risk. For example, if someone is afraid of looking dumb, find ways to make sure he is knowledgeable about the initiative before talking about it in front of his team, or work with the team to become encouraging and supportive.

- *See: Start Conversations; Facilitate Meetings*

Trust

Where you have found a lack of trust, you either need to work to restore trust in that individual (whether it is you or someone else), or find someone else who is trusted to carry the message. Go to great lengths to maintain your own integrity and help leaders protect theirs.

- *See: Boost Your Power; Gain Leadership Support; Start Conversations*

Resources

When resources are the primary concern, analyze the situation to see if the problem might also stem from motivation (prioritizing other projects ahead of supporting your change initiative), fear (of delegation) or skills (inefficiency), and address those appropriately. If time or money are truly the issue, consider creative alternatives to make supporting your initiative achievable.

- *See: Structural Influence*

Organizational Resistance

The best way to reduce organizational resistance is to stop the cycle by calling attention to it. Encourage the group to acknowledge the hidden ways they are maintaining the status quo. Then, find ways to rewire the successes people experience from the status quo. Make undesired behaviors unsuccessful, and create ways to associate desired behaviors with success.

See: Gain Leadership Support; Facilitate Meetings

Before you jump ahead in the workbook, I encourage you to read through it once to get a complete picture of the model and the tools available to you. Then you can make an informed choice about which drivers of change will help you move forward.

We will start with Leadership, by first assigning the roles and relationships that will best lead and manage change. Then, we will explore how to gain the support you need from leaders.

Next, we will dive into the various Structural Influence methods, the tools, programs, and systems you can design to drive change.

Rounding out the workbook is a set of Personal Influence tools you can use to facilitate change.

Leadership

Assign Roles & Relationships

The Three Primary Roles of Change

The typical model for organizational change focuses on leadership. An individual or group at the top of an organization creates a vision, communicates it, gets people on board, and then drives the change. Everyone else in the organization is expected to follow, albeit with some amount of resistance that will eventually be negated by leaders' determination. I call this the Leadership Model (Figure 5.1.a).

Usually, that's not how change happens. Instead, an individual or group is responsible for implementing the change without really having the authority to get it done. These are the change agents: Individuals within an organization who influence change without authority. Change agents either step forward to impact change or are delegated by leaders to take care of it. Either way, they end up with an indirect relationship with both leaders and employees. This is the Change Agent Model (Figure 5.1.b).

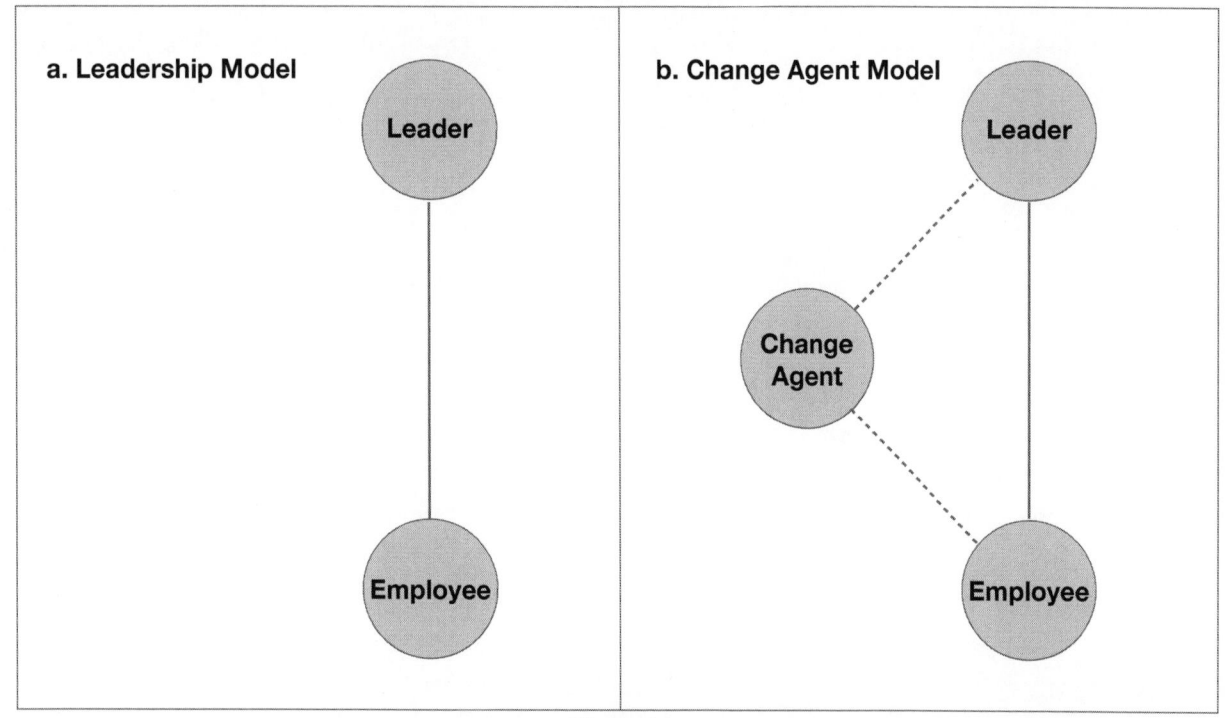

Figure 5.1

Irresistible Change Guide

There are three primary roles that people take on during organizational change, as indicated in Figure 5.1.b. In *Managing at the Speed of Change*, Daryl Conner introduced them as Target, Sponsor and Agent. I prefer to call them Employee, Leader, and Change Agent, respectively. In this chapter, we will identify the people who fill these roles, and determine how you want them to interact in relationship with each other, in order to cohesively influence change.

Employee

The Employee is an individual or group of people within the organization whom you would like to influence to change. The Employee is someone who by the end of the project needs to change the way they work in order for it to be successful.

Leader

The Leader is someone who has authority within the scope of the change. Typically, the Employees work for them or fall below them on the org chart. In the Leadership Model, they take on responsibility for driving change; in the Change Agent Model, they may take more of a supporting or passive role.

Change Agent

The Change Agent is the person or team responsible for getting results, even though the Employees do not work directly for them. They typically fit the description of project managers, although their title may be something else — think human resources, IT, process improvement, engineering, or strategic planning, for example. Anyone who is trying to change the way people work from outside of a traditional line of authority is a change agent.

The main challenge in implementing change with the Change Agent Model instead of the Leadership Model comes down to authority; while Change Agents are often seen as driving the change, Employees take their cues for how to operate from Leaders, specifically their immediate supervisors. When Change Agents and Leaders are misaligned, change stalls.

At the same time, the Change Agent fills a crucial function, even if it makes relationships a bit more challenging. Leaders often don't have the time or the expertise to effectively implement change. Having a dedicated Change Agent position keeps the focus on change, and when effectively backed by Leaders, it demonstrates that the organization is committed to change.

The relationships within an organization are not really as simple as a single triangle. For one change initiative, there are usually multiple triangles that often overlap. Take the following example in Figure 5.2. The CEO is the Leader of the entire organization (a), and is also the direct boss for the department heads (b). Each department head then forms a triangle with his or her own department (c). Even more triangles might define the relationships with managers further down the line. What's more, one person can be the Change Agent for an initiative they are responsible for implementing, while at the same time he or she is the Employee and/or the Leader for other projects happening within the department they work in and manage.

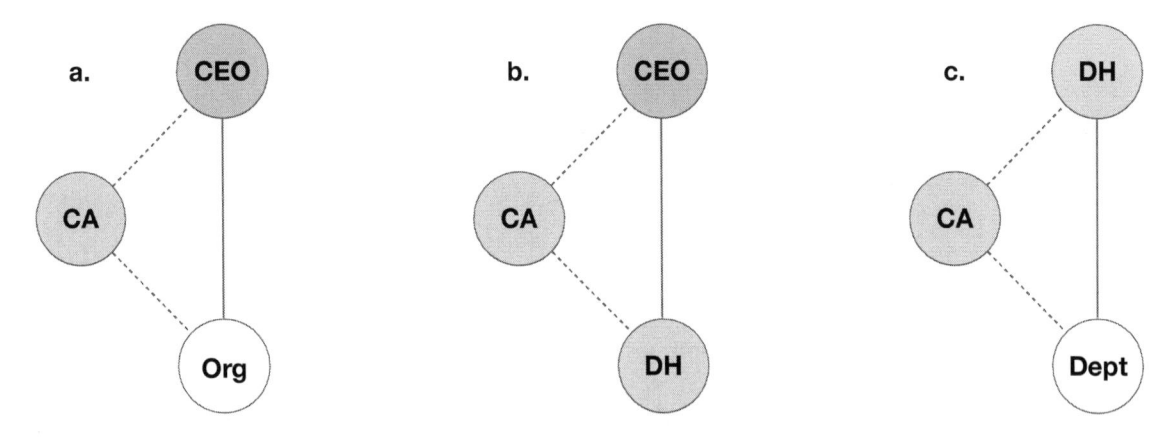

Figure 5.2

In the chart on the next page, list some of the key triangle relationships in your organization. Identify individuals or groups that fill each role. Each row describes one triangle.

First, list the various employees or groups of employees that must change the way they work in order to implement your initiative. Like in the Clarify the Change chapter, the following are some ways you might segment the organization:

Organization Level
Split the organization by title: executives, upper-management, middle-management, supervisors, front-line employees.

Departments, Functional Areas or Business Units
Group people by the task they have in relation to your initiative, or by natural organizational boundaries.

Regional or Geography
Divide the organization by regions or languages.

Union or Non-Union
Split employees between those in a bargaining unit and those that are not.

Next, identify the leaders who have authority with each of the groups in the Employee column. The leaders may be the direct boss of the Employee, or may skip layers of the organization. Organizations with matrix reporting structures may have multiple leaders for the same employee group.

Then, assign the change agent for each relationship. It may be you, someone else on your team, or another person in the organization who is in the best position to play that role. If there are any Employee - Leader relationships that you expect to not have direct involvement with a change agent, write "None" in the Change Agent column.

It may help to draw a diagram of the triangles to show how they overlap and connect. There is room underneath the chart for you to do that.

Key Triangle Relationships Chart

	Employee	Leader	Change Agent
1			
2			
3			
4			
5			
6			
7			

Diagram:

Now, let's take a closer look at each of the three primary roles of change and how they each play a unique role in organizational change. Then, we will explore how the roles interact with each other. For each triangle you have identified, we will assign roles and relationships that will best manage the change together.

The Role of a Change Agent

A person who implements organizational change must wear many different hats. Effective change agents demonstrate extraordinary versatility within a broad skill set. The following are some of the roles you may play as you influence change in your organization.

The Detective

Implementing change is rarely as straightforward as executing obvious activities. Dealing with people's behaviors and attitudes usually requires digging below the surface to understand the dynamics of the organization. Change agents look for clues that give away what is really preventing change from happening, so they can determine the steps most likely to remove obstacles and bring about success. The Detective is observant and analytical.

The Advocate

Every organizational change needs someone who speaks up in favor of it and keeps attention on it. Change agents gain support for the initiative and engage people to participate. They also keep beating the drum of change when everyone else is busy with other activities. The Advocate is vocal and persistent.

The Counselor

Change happens when individuals alter their own activities, behaviors and attitudes. People experience varied emotions as their sense of stability is removed. In most cases, they are required to take risks and step outside their comfort zones. As a change agent, understand the personal implications of people involved, so you can help people feel better about making the changes. The Counselor listens and encourages.

The Facilitator

One of the key activities of a change agent is finding ways to help people change. Change agents clarify the change and make it easier to perform. As a facilitator, you design systems, tools, forms, and processes to enable people to succeed as they go through change. The Facilitator is helpful and creative.

The Mediator

Different groups and individuals undergoing change in an organization frequently have opposing priorities. Change agents manage conflict by helping different parties see the situation from the other's point of view, and by finding common goals. They work to improve understanding and reduce friction between multiple parties so they can collaborate to implement change. The Mediator is a peacemaker.

The Expert

Change agents rely on their expertise to build their authority within the organization. By sharing knowledge, they demonstrate that they can be relied upon to point people in the right direction. Sometimes knowledge transfer occurs directly through training, but it also happens every day in meetings and conversations. The Expert is confident and knowledgeable.

The Law
A change agent ensures that there are goals, targets, and due dates for the project. Then they keep people on track to achieve them. Change agents find ways to hold people accountable, and make sure that appropriate rewards — or corrections — are handed out as necessary. The Law is determined and conscientious.

As you implement change in your organization, pay attention to the change agent roles you play most often, and which you feel most comfortable filling. Select which hat will make you most effective in different situations. As you increase your versatility, you will improve your effectiveness as a change agent.

The Role of a Leader
Successful organizational change depends on leaders — managers and bosses who have direct authority with people going through the change — to support and execute change in their span of influence. Effective leaders acknowledge that their support is crucial to success and commit to doing their part. The following are some of the roles leaders may play as they drive change in your organization.

The Sponsor
Leaders act as advocates for the change at their level in the organization. They are representatives who keep the change in front of their peers, the "higher-ups." A Sponsor is the person who won't let the change initiative die from lack of attention or resources, and is willing to use his political capital to make the change happen. The Sponsor is the champion.

The Role Model
Leaders of change must be willing to go first. They demonstrate the behaviors and attitudes that are expected of everyone else. Employees watch leaders for consistency between words and actions to see if they should believe the change is really going to happen. The Role Model is self-aware and deliberate.

The Decision-Maker
As managers, leaders usually control resources such as people, budgets, and equipment, and thus have the authority to make decisions that affect the initiative. They have the ability to say "yes" or "no" to the project moving forward within the span of their control. During change, leaders must leverage their decision-making authority and choose the options that will support the initiative. The Decision-Maker is decisive and sets priorities that support change.

The Voice
Leaders are the face and the voice of change. They communicate often to share information, keep people updated and offer encouragement. When employees hear multiple messages in the organization, the one they listen to the most is their immediate boss. Leaders interpret the change message to be relevant for their reports, while still matching the overall message. The Voice is transparent and consistent.

The Motivator
Leaders provide the motivation to change. They create a sense of urgency and importance about the change, and show commitment and passion about getting things done. They offer recognition to those who

are participating and doing well. Leaders realize that change can be difficult, and understand the need for people to be motivated to step out of their comfort zone. The Motivator is energetic and empathetic.

The Enforcer

With their authority, leaders hold people in the organization accountable for the change. They uphold agreements and make sure others do the same. They don't let people get away with not changing, and work to understand the underlying reasons so they can remove obstacles. Leaders follow through on delivering consequences when people don't do their part. The Enforcer is exacting and fair.

Effective leaders recognize that change cannot happen unless they fulfill the roles that only those in authority can. Enlist their support and clarify the roles you need them to fill in their areas and in different situations. Help leaders in your organization see the importance of the unique part they play in change.

The Role of an Employee

While much of this workbook focuses on the influence of the Change Agent and Leader, those who are changing their work also play a role that should not be diminished. Their role is not to simply change (as much as you might prefer it). The following are productive roles that the Employee might play during change implementation.

The Volunteer

Some employees acknowledge the need for change and are even enthusiastic about the prospect of it. They readily volunteer to get involved and become de facto Change Agents. Enlist people who believe in the change, and also those who like to control things. Letting people help is a great way to get them to own the change. The Volunteer is engaged and enthusiastic.

The Reflector

Employees need to be aware of the affect the change is having on them, and be able to communicate feedback to change agents and leaders. They honestly reflect their change experience, and share what works and what doesn't. Convert skeptics — those who question the validity of the change or the resolve to make it happen — into Reflectors who tell you examples that their skepticism is justified. The Reflector is thoughtful and offers constructive feedback.

The Participant

Employees who accept the change without being involved are Participants. They are willing to try it, incorporate it into their jobs, and move on. For this initiative, these employees are followers, in the sense that they are ready to go along with what leaders and change agents influence them to do. The Participant is focused on execution.

Organizational change ultimately occurs at an individual level, and so the transition of each Employee to the future state is the final determinant of the success of your initiative. In order for Employees to incorporate specific changes into their work, they need to properly go through the process of change. The role the Employee plays depends on their level of engagement, as influenced by the Leader and the Change Agent.

The Relationships of Change

The primary roles of change do not work independently from each other. On the contrary — the roles work in full view of each other, are influenced by each other, and collaborate with each other... or not. Defining the expectations between the roles is essential to success but often overlooked.

In the Change Agent Model triangle, there are three relationships (the lines between the roles). As indicated in Figure 5.3 below, there are two roles for each relationship. The arrows going both ways show that there are expectations of both roles in each relationship.

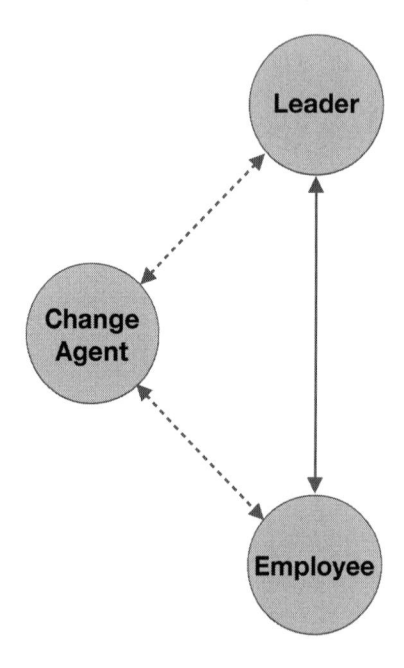

Figure 5.3

The relationships described below follow a general model for who should do what during change. Your organization may be different. There is some flexibility in the balance of relationships that will end in success, depending on the skills and expertise of the individuals, the culture of the organization as it relates to authority, the structure of the organization, and what your initiative is. Later on, you will have the chance to define the roles and relationships for your initiative.

Leader → Employee

The Leader of the change is viewed as the owner or at least strong advocate of the project from the point of view of the Employee. They are tasked with motivating the Employee to implement the change, and with holding them accountable for doing so. The Leader provides the answer to "Why are we doing this?" by sharing the vision and creating a sense of urgency. Although the Change Agent may orchestrate communication between the Leader and Employee, the Leader should usually be the messenger, especially to direct reports.

Employee → Leader

During change, the Employee listens, participates, and tries to meet goals and expectations. They ask questions when they don't understand the message and speak up when they see an obstacle approaching.

Change Agent → Employee

The Change Agent provides the Employee with the means of changing. This may include education, training, tools, and information. The Change Agent answers the question, "How are we going to change?" The Change Agent is in a good spot to receive feedback on the change from the Employee; since the Change Agent doesn't have direct authority, there is less perceived risk of speaking up.

Employee → Change Agent

The Employee gets involved by volunteering to help the Change Agent implement the change in their area. They provide feedback and offer solutions to obstacles.

Change Agent → Leader

Besides taking on many of the tasks involved with the change initiative, the primary role of the Change Agent with regard to the Leader is to provide feedback. Feedback takes the form of both objective information, such as survey results or progress reviews, and more personal observations that show the Leader how well he is performing the Leader role. There is no one better suited to see what the Leader is doing to inadvertently sabotage the change than the Change Agent. The expectation of feedback should be built into the Change Agent – Leader relationship from the outset. If avoided, the balance of the change triangle may be permanently disrupted.

Leader → Change Agent

While the Change Agent is responsible for making the change happen, the Leader must provide his support for the change by fulfilling the expectations of the Leader role. The Leader also uses his authority on behalf of the Change Agent, and in some cases may delegate authority to the Change Agent. We will cover the topic of leadership support in depth in the next chapter.

Next, we will apply these concepts and determine the roles and relationships for your change initiative.

Assign Roles and Relationships

Using the Change Agent Model triangle structure, we will now describe who fills each role for your change initiative and how they relate to one another. On the page that follows these instructions, complete one diagram for each of the main triangle relationships you identified in the Key Triangle Relationships Chart.

In each of the circles, list the names of individuals or groups who fill the Employee, Leader and Change Agent roles for this particular triangle relationship.

Then, starting in the lower righthand corner, describe the key expected behaviors and mindsets for the Employee. For the change to be a success, what new ways of working must they incorporate into their jobs?

Next, identify the ways the Leader can best support and influence the Employee to incorporate those behaviors and mindsets into their work. Use the key roles of a leader described earlier in this chapter to help narrow the list. Be specific about the ways the Leader can help drive the change, and also how they can empower the Employee to take ownership of the change.

Now, list the ways the Change Agent can support and influence both the Employee and the Leader to do their parts. How might you get each role to do what you've just listed? How can you help them succeed in their roles? What might you do or create to move them in that direction? What feedback or other information might you provide? Use the key roles of a change agent described in this chapter to give you some ideas. The better you can define the Change Agent role and how it supports the Leader and the Employee, the more you will be seen as an enabler than a meddler.

Last, add the ways the Leader and the Employee connect back to the Change Agent to help drive change forward. How can each role help you help them? What feedback or other information can they provide? How can they participate in implementing the change? Incorporating the roles of Leader and Employee into the change process itself will go a long way towards building ownership and reducing resistance.

If your overlapping relationship triangles contain multiple layers of the organization — for example, a department (Employee) and the department head (Leader) in one triangle and the department heads (Employee) and business unit manager (Leader) in another, and on up the line — start this exercise from the lowest level of the organization chart and work your way up. Like pieces to a puzzle, match up the ways Leaders support and influence change from other charts with the expectations when the same group is listed as an Employee. That way, you can see the line of influence and support from the top to the bottom of the organization.

Roles and Relationships Diagram

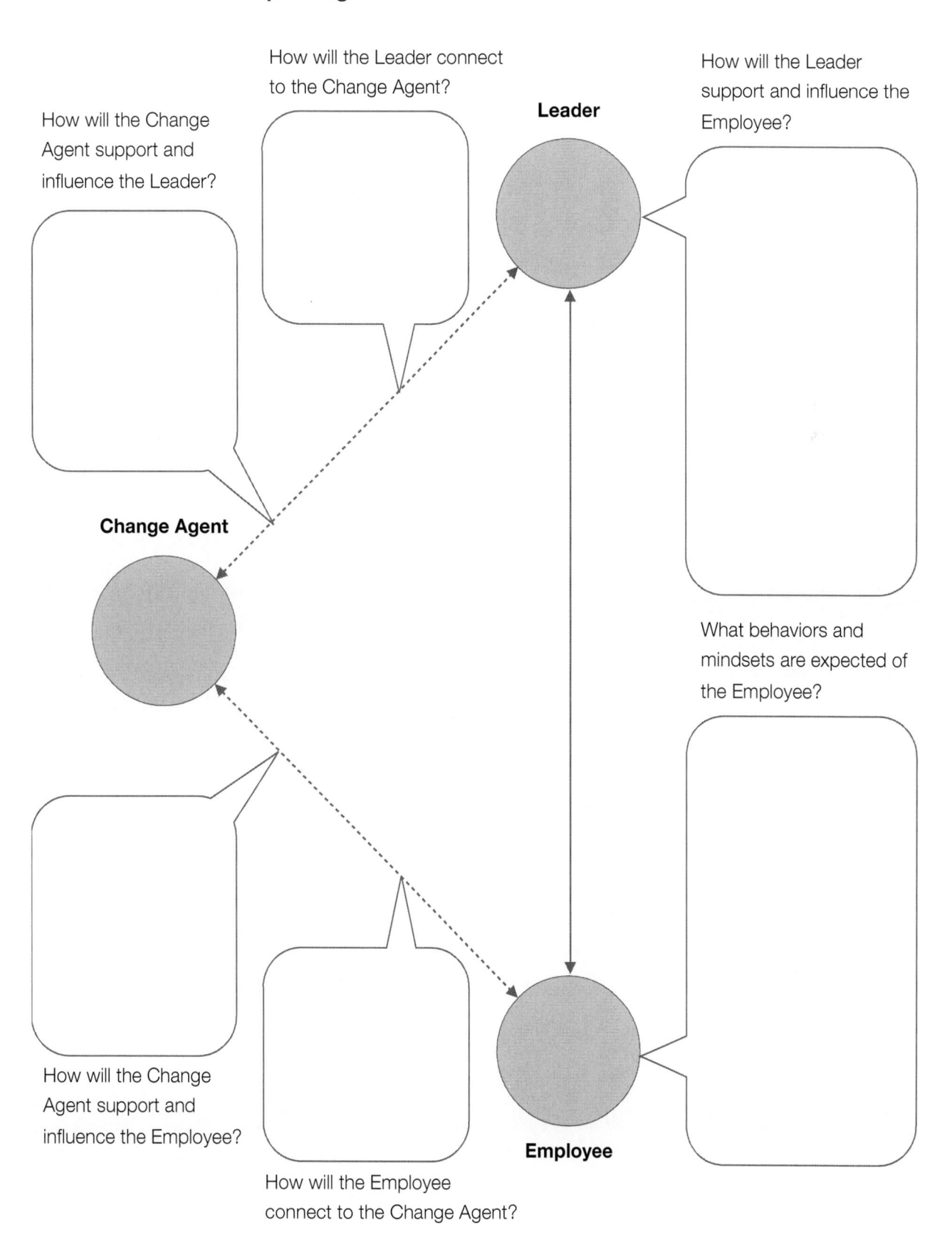

How will the Change Agent support and influence the Leader?

How will the Leader connect to the Change Agent?

Leader

How will the Leader support and influence the Employee?

Change Agent

What behaviors and mindsets are expected of the Employee?

How will the Change Agent support and influence the Employee?

How will the Employee connect to the Change Agent?

Employee

Irresistible Change Guide

Enable the Key Change Roles

Having clear roles and relationships for your change initiative will go a long way towards managing the change smoothly. When people don't know how to best interact or what their responsibility is, things can fall through the cracks. Clarifying relationships up front can help make difficult conversations easier because there is already an expectation that they will happen.

Use these Roles and Relationships Diagrams to start the conversation about how the change will be led and managed going forward. Invite people to define their personal role in the change initiative. Discuss how you will address when roles get murky, or when individuals appear to be shirking or contradicting their change role. Being deliberate about assigning change roles and relationships, while uncomfortable at first, will help ensure that things are less awkward down the road.

Once you identify the roles and relationships of the key people involved in the change initiative, make sure everyone understands and agrees to filling those roles. Refer back to the relationship diagrams and update them when anything occurs that requires clarification of who does what. The triangle relationships of change are a delicate balance of authority and responsibility that need to be managed deliberately to enable your change.

Now that you know how leaders can best influence and support your change initiative, in the next chapter, we will zoom in on how to gain and maintain the support of individual leaders in your organization. And later on, we will determine what tools and systems you can create to help people incorporate the changes into their work. We will also work on ways you can exert your personal influence when your initiative calls for it.

Gain Leadership Support

The Importance of Leadership Support

It almost goes without saying that an organizational change initiative without proper levels of leadership support is doomed to fail. Perhaps the project will be paid lip service, but it will ultimately either be ignored into oblivion or cut short of its potential with one drop of the axe.

Not only do organizational leaders have the power to make or break your project on their own, but it is impossible to skip over them to change the part of the organization over which they have authority. Individuals experiencing change will look to those in power for confirmation that they are committed to the new way of doing things. It is under intense scrutiny that leaders are watched to see if their actions match their intentions. If not, the change initiative will be dismissed as "flavor of the month" and not taken seriously.

Amid all this doom and gloom, there is a bright side. *You don't have to settle for the level of leadership support you currently have.* As fellow human beings, leaders are capable of being informed and influenced, just like anyone else in your organization.

Gaining leadership support is not just something that you have to do at the beginning of a project. Maintaining support is a continual job for change agents. Follow the steps in the rest of this chapter to gain the support you need, in the beginning and throughout your initiative.

Four Signs Leaders Don't Really Support Your Change

As a change agent, once the change initiative expands beyond your own span of influence, you need to rely on leaders in the organization to carry the change forward. Without their full support, the change fizzles. The trouble is, leaders often don't properly support change even when they agree that it should happen.

The following are four things leaders do that indicate they may not fully support your change:

Exhibiting behaviors that work against change

Often leaders claim that they are on board with change, but their words and actions indicate otherwise. Sometimes, it's a lack of self-awareness; they don't see how the organizational change requires their own personal change or departmental change. They may see it as applying to and affecting everyone else but them. At other times, it's a more deliberate resistance. Either way, if their behaviors aren't better aligned with the change, the people who work for them will soon doubt the change themselves.

Blaming employees for not changing
Some leaders expect the worst up front. They don't even want to try to change their area for fear of resistance or even sabotage by those who work for them. There are at least two things that may be going on in this situation. The leader may not believe in the change himself, and is projecting his own doubts on his department. Or, the leader may not have enough faith in his own leadership abilities to implement the changes. Leaders who expect defeat create a self-fulfilling prophecy.

Doing change their own way
When multiple leaders sponsor the change, employees end up feeling like they are the rope in a game of tug-of-war. Which leaders are present in the room determines the direction the change is going that day. Employees and change agents feel compelled to go in multiple directions, resulting in scope creep and wasted time. When multiple leaders send conflicting messages, it's time to clarify the change and get some agreement.

Maintaining fiefdoms
Large changes usually require cross-functional collaboration by leaders. In the face of change, some leaders instead protect their departments and hoard their power. They become unwilling to share information and refuse to accept and apply outside ideas. In other words, they entrench their silos in an attempt to avoid change.

One of your greatest opportunities to influence the organization lies in getting the proper support of leaders for your change initiative. Watch for signs that leaders are not really supporting the change and then resolve to do something about it.

Identify Leadership

Before you can come up with a plan for raising support for your initiative, you need to know whose support you need to raise. When we use the term "Leadership," it typically means the group of people whose titles reside at the top of the org chart. However, the list may be different for the transformation you are trying to achieve.

The key is to decouple the nebulous term "Leadership" from the names of individuals who can impact your project. Since each leader has his own opinions, knowledge and motivations, it is important to treat these people as individuals, and not as a faceless group.

List All Possible Leaders
We start this exercise by identifying all those individuals in the organization who might have a significant impact on the success of your initiative. Start by thinking of people who fit in the following categories:

The Obvious
In the last chapter, you already identified those people who have authority with the employees you would like to influence. These are the members of the organization that come to mind when you think of leadership. Include those members of management who you consider your most immediate superiors, like your boss and your boss's boss. Also select those members who impact your change initiative directly and indirectly.

- Who do you typically include as part of leadership from your point of view?
- Who owns the processes or departments affected by the change?

Decision Makers

You will need the support of individuals with decision-making authority for the factors affecting your change initiative. Decision makers may not have been in your triangle diagrams in the last chapter, because they may not have direct reporting relationships with those going through the change. Nevertheless, they control a piece of your project and you need their support.

- Who are the decision makers who have a stake in your initiative?
- Which individuals have the ability to say "yes" or "no" to each aspect of your project?
- Who has the power to provide funding for your initiative?

Influencers

Some true leaders in your organization do not hold leadership or management titles. These individuals can sometimes have a greater impact on how a change initiative is perceived in the organization than management. Others look to these employees to fill in the information gaps and to help them form opinions.

- Who has considerable influence on the people who would be affected by the change?
- Who are your informal leaders?

Consider the administrative assistant who is the hub of information. Look for individuals that people flock to for help, or who volunteer to write for the corporate newsletter. Watch for these and other opinion leaders to find your potential influencers.

Snipers

Least obvious are the people you are likely to ignore: those who have nothing much to do with your project, and who don't really care about it, but who have the power or influence to affect the outcome.

- Who might kill your initiative simply by saying or doing the wrong thing?
- Who do you wish would just stay out of the way?

For example, consider a high-level executive who occasionally helicopters into the office, catches wind of the project, and makes an immediate and uninformed judgment about the project, effectively derailing it.

Identify the leaders involved in your initiative and list them in the chart on the next page. Include name, title, and the impact each is expected to have on your initiative.

Leader List

Name	Title	Expected Impact on Change

Assign Levels of Support

Before you garner support for your initiative from the Leader List, consider that there are different levels of support. We often interchange the term buy-in for support, but really buy-in is the minimum amount of support required to be called support at all. As you will see, there are two other forms of support that are more valuable than simple buy-in.

In this section, you will learn the different levels of support and then identify where each leader is currently and where they need to be in order for your initiative to succeed. The list will help you prioritize which leaders have the most support to raise, and which leaders need the most attention from you.

Five Levels of Leadership Support

All support for your initiative is not created equal. You will need different levels of support from different individuals. There are roughly five levels of support, defined as follows:

Ownership

An initiative owner takes personal responsibility for the success or failure of the initiative. He or she plans, communicates and holds people accountable for task completion.

As the change agent for this initiative, you may consider yourself the owner; however, if your ownership is temporary and someone else will take over the operation after the implementation, then you will need that person to claim ownership in order for it to continue after you move on.

The number of people who need to claim ownership of the initiative will depend on the scope of the project. You can have multiple people with ownership if accountability is independent. For example, if each department head will have the same responsibility for the implementation within his own department, then you might want each of them to support the project as an owner.

Commitment

People who are committed to your initiative demonstrate it by taking action in favor of it. They are invested in bringing about a positive outcome. They do not own the project per se, but they do their part to make it happen.

Commitment is sufficient for individuals who will not be planning the initiative or holding others accountable for the outcome. It is the minimum requirement of anyone who is expected to take action to move the initiative forward.

Buy-in

In the game of poker, "buy-in" is the amount you pay just to join the game. When you have people's buy-in, it means they may agree with you, but may not act on it.

At best, people who exhibit buy-in are your cheerleaders. You may only need their verbal support because it is out of the scope of their job to take action to support your initiative. In that case, buy-in is sufficient.

At worst, buy-in without commitment is like someone who does not "walk the talk." They may honestly agree with your initiative, but they do not take the appropriate action to move the project forward.

Neutral

These are the people who don't really care about your initiative. They either are not affected or are just along for the ride. Watch out for snipers in this category — people who are out of the loop, but if they suddenly join the loop, they may derail your progress.

Opposition

Unfortunately, there will be people who don't agree with your initiative and demonstrate outright resistance to it. There are different levels of opposition, from relatively benign disagreement to downright belligerent and argumentative. For the sake of this workbook, we include all leaders who oppose the project into one category.

Assess and Assign Levels of Support

Each leader you identify is currently demonstrating a certain level of support for your initiative. Likewise, each individual has a specific role they will need to play in order for your change initiative to succeed.

In the Leadership Support Chart on the next page, list the key people you identified in the Leader List for your project. Then, chart the current and desired levels of support for each individual on your list.

Leadership Support Chart

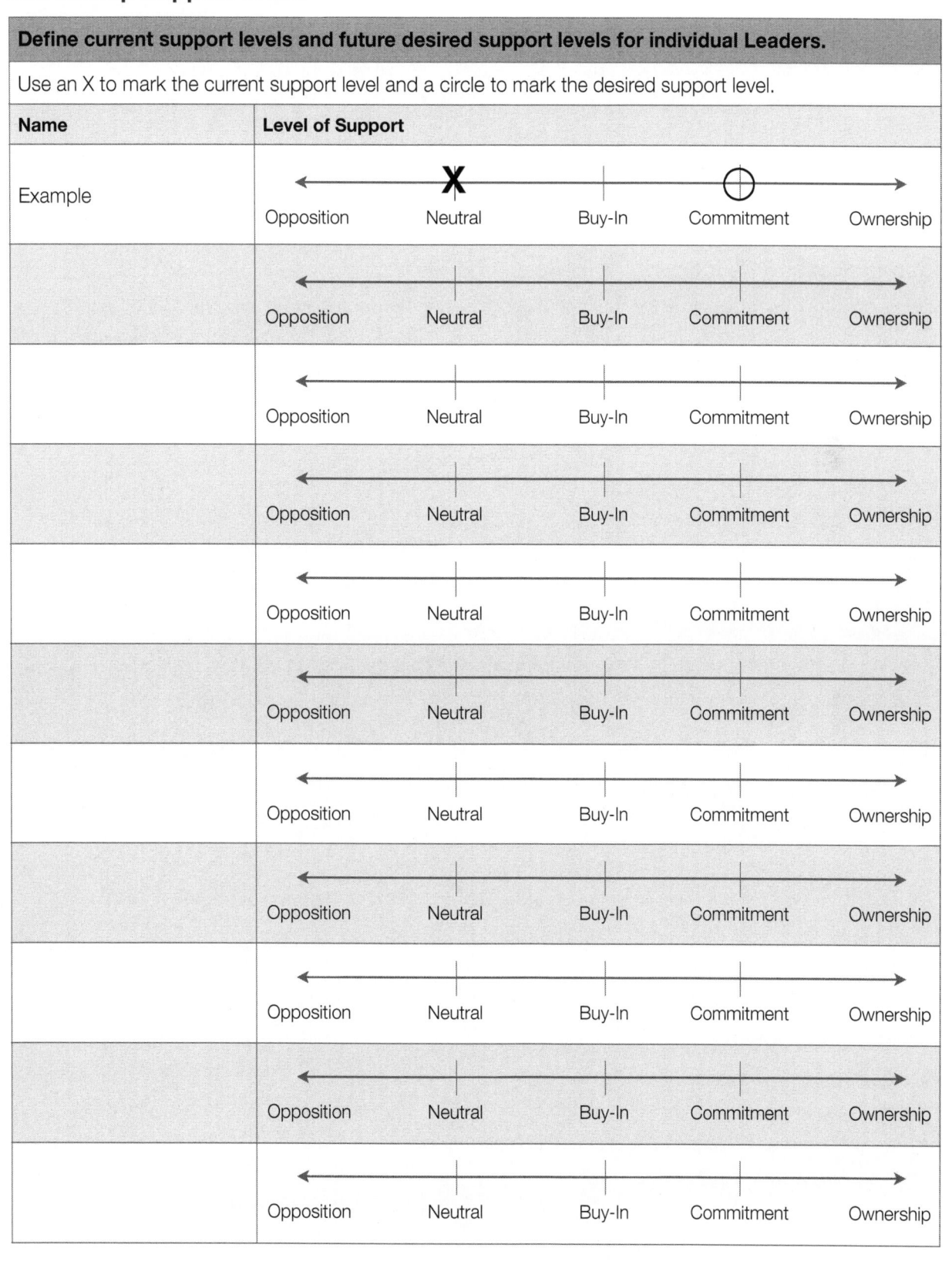

Define current support levels and future desired support levels for individual Leaders.

Use an X to mark the current support level and a circle to mark the desired support level.

Name	Level of Support
Example	Opposition — Neutral (X) — Buy-In — Commitment (O) — Ownership
	Opposition — Neutral — Buy-In — Commitment — Ownership
	Opposition — Neutral — Buy-In — Commitment — Ownership
	Opposition — Neutral — Buy-In — Commitment — Ownership
	Opposition — Neutral — Buy-In — Commitment — Ownership
	Opposition — Neutral — Buy-In — Commitment — Ownership
	Opposition — Neutral — Buy-In — Commitment — Ownership
	Opposition — Neutral — Buy-In — Commitment — Ownership
	Opposition — Neutral — Buy-In — Commitment — Ownership
	Opposition — Neutral — Buy-In — Commitment — Ownership
	Opposition — Neutral — Buy-In — Commitment — Ownership

Determine Expectations

You already have a general idea of what level of support you need from each key leader. Now we are going to start talking about each person individually. The goal is to identify specifically what your initiative needs each leader to do to support the change.

You do not gain support by asking, "Do I have your support?" The answer you get may be "Yes," but you still may not get what you need in the form of words and actions. First, define what it means for each person to support your project, so you can make sure each one does what is really needed.

Identify Desired Processes, Behaviors, and Mindsets

Each leader is in a unique position in the organization. They make decisions, talk to others, and influence followers. Using the Four Layers of Change concept, your initiative would be more successful if leaders performed certain processes, exhibited certain behaviors, and conveyed and, ideally, held certain mindsets that would lead to the desired outcome. Performing these processes, behaviors and mindsets are the way leaders demonstrate support for the initiative.

Processes

Processes are a set of activities or tasks that need to be completed. For example, if ABC Corp, the fictitious organization we discussed earlier, has an outcome goal to increase innovation, then an activity that a leader might be expected to do is hold a regular meeting with employees to collect and track ideas.

Behaviors

Behaviors are the manner in which leaders perform the processes. In the same ABC Corp example, leaders might need to ask employees for ideas without passing immediate judgment on the ideas.

Mindsets

Mindsets are the way leaders feel when they perform the processes and behaviors, supported by their beliefs. The leaders mentioned above need to believe that their employees' suggestions are worth listening to.

The leaders on your list also have existing processes, behaviors and mindsets that may differ from the desired ones. In addition to what you need each leader to start doing, consider what he needs to stop doing, or what you want to make sure he doesn't start doing. Looking for the positive, identify the processes, behaviors and mindsets that he already does that you want him to continue to do.

On the next page, complete one Detailed Expectations Table for each prioritized leader with the key processes, behaviors, and mindsets that he needs to start, stop and continue doing to best support your initiative. Don't worry about getting the categories correct. The categories are meant to help you think beyond tasks and start thinking about underlying motivations.

Detailed Expectations Table

Name:

What does this person need to *start* doing?		
Processes	Behaviors	Mindsets

What does this person need to *continue* doing?		
Processes	Behaviors	Mindsets

What does this person need to *stop* doing, or not do?		
Processes	Behaviors	Mindsets

Identify Resistance to Support

You have identified the best case scenario mindsets, behaviors and processes for each leader on the list. Using the same approach introduced in the Uncover Resistance chapter, we will now explore what is preventing each leader from doing those things now, and keeping each from demonstrating the support you need to succeed. The goal is to identify what is missing so you can fill the gap by designing influence methods in the next section.

Sources of Resistance to Demonstrating Support

Let's look at each of the eight sources of personal resistance as they pertain to the leaders on your list. Consider these factors when looking for the discrepancy in current and desired support, and complete the Individual Resistance Assessment on the next page for each leader.

Valid Concerns

The leader may have valid concerns about your initiative, causing him to oppose or at least hold back from fully supporting it.

- What concerns does he have?

Information

The leader may lack knowledge of the details of the project, such as benefits. Also, he may not know what is expected of him.

- What might he not know or understand?

Skills

The leader may need additional knowledge or training in order to know how to complete the activity or behavior. The change initiative might require technological skills, or the leader may lack leadership skills such as holding people accountable or communication skills.

- What might he be unable to do?

Motivation

The project or the necessary behaviors may not be aligned with what the leader considers to be his or his team's best interests.

- What does he prioritize ahead of the change initiative?

Power

When a leader is not allowed to show the desired support there is a power gap. It may be real; for example, if his boss doesn't support it, he might feel that he can't. It may be perceived; the project may go against organizational culture, or there may be feared repercussions for supporting the initiative.

- Who has control?

Fear

Change by definition means taking a risk by doing something different from what probably has brought success in the past. Asking a leader to perform new activities and behaviors may conjure up fear of failure, fear of being wrong, fear of looking stupid, fear of losing power, among many others. The change may also be perceived as a potential threat.

- What might he be avoiding?

Trust

The leader may lack trust, either with higher-up leaders, with his peers, with his team of direct reports, or perhaps even with you.

- Who or what might he doubt?

Resources

Time and money constraints factor into decisions for which activities the leader will complete and support. However, lack of resources is an easy excuse, and is sometimes a symptom of another barrier to support.

- What may be his constraint?

For each leader you identified, complete the Individual Resistance Assessment on the next page. Start with the key expectations from the Detailed Expectations Table for that leader. Next, describe the symptoms of resistance that prompted you to assign him the current (lacking) level of support. Then, identify which factors are most likely standing in the way of the full support you need.

Individual Resistance Assessment

Name:

Expectations

Symptoms of Resistance

Potential Sources of Personal Resistance	
Valid Concerns	Power
Information	Fear
Skills	Trust
Motivation	Resources

Reduce Resistance to Support

The last step is to determine how to reduce or remove the resistance to support you identified in the previous step. Then, it is up to you to take concrete steps to secure the support you need for your change initiative.

Building on the sources of resistance in the last section, let's determine how best to remove or reduce them. For each of the sources of resistance you identified, answer the following questions to gain some insights about what steps you can take to close the gap between the support you want and the support you have.

Valid Reasons
- How might you help him through it?

Information
- What does he need to know?
- How might you communicate it?

Skills
- What training might be provided?

Motivation
- How might you align the initiative with his values and best interests?
- What incentives might be created or eliminated?

Power
- Who might hold him accountable or empower him to take appropriate action?

Fear
- How might you reduce his perceived risk?

Trust
- How might you repair relationships?
- What might you do to prove the change will work?

Resources
- Where might he find more resources?

Based on the resistance to support you identified for each leader in the last section, write down the ideas that come to mind for how to reduce resistance and influence him to take on the new processes, behaviors and mindsets. Create one list of ideas for each leader using the chart on the next page.

Later on in this workbook, you will learn more influence methods you can also apply to gaining leadership support.

Ideas to Gain Support

Name:

Desired Result	Source of Resistance	Actions to Reduce Resistance

Three Traps that Stop Change Agents from Getting the Support They Need

It is common knowledge that in order for your change initiative to grow beyond your own span of influence you need leadership buy-in. The truth is you need much more than approval; as a change agent you need leaders in your organization to take action that supports your initiative.

The trouble is, leaders often don't do what is needed to implement change, even if they agree it should happen. You may think, If only they would (fill in the blank), you would be able to make some real progress.

This lack of proper leadership support is the top challenge for most change agents. It frequently stays that way because change agents get stuck by the following traps.

"It's not my place."
Allison was a supervisor who had been given a special assignment to implement the recommendations that resulted from an employee survey. The biggest roadblock to improvement, she decided, was her boss's boss, the very person who had commissioned the survey. Allison's boss agreed but would not do anything about it. "What can I do?" Allison asked, "It's not my place to address the issues with my boss's boss."

The organizational hierarchy can seem like an insurmountable hurdle over which to affect change. When the person whose support you need is outside of one degree of authority, it can seem like political suicide to attempt to do something about it. From this position of helplessness, it is easy to get stuck hoping he will figure it out on his own.

"That's just the way they are."
Dan was a senior manager who worked directly for the CEO. Dan's key initiative to improve the company was to develop and solidify accountability to procedures. The CEO, while supporting the initiative verbally, did not want to abide by procedures himself. It was the CEO who had embodied the previously lackadaisical culture. "I can't do anything about it. That's just the way he is," Dan lamented.

We often assume that the behaviors of others reflect an inner character trait. This assumption is so common that psychologists call it the fundamental attribution error. When you consider that someone will not support you because it is part of his DNA, of course you would automatically chalk it up as a lost cause. You get trapped knowing it is impossible to change someone else.

"He just doesn't like me."
John was a project manager who needed key data from the manager of another department. However, John's phone calls and e-mails requesting the information were repeatedly ignored. John asked his boss to request the same information, and it was immediately handed over. "Maybe she just doesn't like me," was John's reasoning.

This trap is the mirror image of the fundamental attribution error. Instead of thinking the lack of support is caused by her character, you think the lack of support is your own fault. Whenever you interpret her behavior as a personal slight - she doesn't respect you, she doesn't like you, she doesn't trust you - it traps you with self-doubt. Insecurity is a lousy place from which to exert influence as a change agent.

Allison, Dan and John are composites of real change agents who were stuck. But none of their traps were inherently real. The traps were assumptions they made about the leaders and the organization.

The first step in getting out of a trap is to recognize that you may be in one. Separate the facts from your assumptions about them. From there, you can select a new point of view and step out of the trap, so you can find new ways to get the support you need to implement change.

Structural Influence

Structural Influence

Five Fundamental Levers of Influence

Influencing organizational change is undoubtedly a complicated endeavor. You have to assess your unique situation and determine when and how to use the vast array of influence techniques at your disposal. And yet, patterns appear when you look at what you are really trying to do when you influence others. Underlying all your options are five fundamental levers of influence you can apply to accomplish your goals. Anything you do to influence others will employ at least one of these levers.

Provide Clarity

In our busy workplaces, messages that don't help us accomplish the task at hand can be easily overlooked. Introducing change adds more chaos and uncertainty to the workplace. To break through the clutter and reduce confusion, provide as much clarity as possible. Raise awareness of the need for change. Clarify expectations by directly communicating them and also by sharing stories and modeling behaviors to demonstrate what employees should do differently. Provide feedback to help people course-correct. Clearly communicate the vision the organization is trying to achieve, and establish goals and deadlines for getting there. Zero in on the key elements that people need to know, do and accomplish so they understand their part in the change initiative.

Enable Progress

Even if people know what to do differently, they still need to be able to do it. Part of influence is enabling people to change. For those whose difficulty with change is internal, help them deal with their fears and emotions by developing support systems and fostering resilience. For others who need to increase their capability to change, build skills, provide tools, and find ways to make it easy. And when the organization itself gets in the way, remove obstacles, adjust the environment, and eliminate any behaviors that hinder change. Enabling people to change means building their personal ability and also removing anything that prevents them from changing.

Build Trust

People choose instinctively who and what will influence them, and the basis for that choice is trust. To directly influence people, they need to trust you. And to implement organizational change, they must also trust the leaders of the organization, their coworkers, and they also must believe the change itself will really work. Remove doubt about the change by addressing objections, respecting resistance, and reducing risk. Generate short-term wins to prove the change will work. Ensure alignment and consistency across the organization to help leaders gain credibility. Show respect, keep your word, and above all listen, while helping others do the same. Trust is a fragile commodity that is difficult to repair, so do whatever you can to build it, not break it.

Invite Participation

Another lever of influence is to involve people so they feel like they own the change. When employees are a part of the change process, they are more likely to advocate for it instead of stand in the way. Involve people in clarifying what needs to change and designing the change process from the beginning. Invite them to participate by asking for ideas and input. Get people together to have conversations they wouldn't otherwise have. Ask for commitment and delegate responsibility for implementing pieces of the initiative. Empower people to make decisions and to take action to achieve the desired results. When people feel they have contributed to the design and implementation of change, they essentially influence themselves.

Motivate Action

Create the necessary energy for change by giving people a reason to participate. Establish a sense of urgency so they understand why things can't stay the way they are now. Inspire them to work towards a common future with a vision that connects to their values. Find the emotional connection, and appeal to logic. Harness peer pressure by showing that others are already participating, and celebrate success. Tap into a range of emotions to spur people forward, from positive ones like pride, joy and hope to negative ones like guilt, anxiety and anger. Encourage, while holding people accountable. Provide the incentive to leave the comfort of the status quo and to exert extra effort to make things better in the future.

In the Structural Influence section and the next section on Personal Influence, we will apply these five fundamental levers of influence to move people towards the desired future state. We will consider the individuals or groups whom you need to influence, select the levers that will best move them in the right direction, and then tailor the ways you will influence change to that unique situation. Apply all five levers of influence over time for maximum impact.

The Tools of Influence

When we think of influence, we usually think of personal influence. Personal influence works at an individual or small group level, where you work with people directly to determine how to best facilitate them through the change. Personal influence consists of nothing but yourself, your power and your relationships, which we will talk about in the next main section.

Organizational change requires another type of influence. Structural influence methods are the tools, programs and other systems you create to help people change. These methods serve several functions that support the change process. As the name implies, structural influence provides structure for the change. These tools add consistency across the organization. They leverage time and money, both yours and the resources of the people going through the change. Each structural influence method you create will apply at least one of the five fundamental levers of influence to help people move in the right direction.

The following are some common structural influence methods:

Tools
- Procedures, forms, checklists and templates

- Data analysis and reports

Programs
- Education and training
- Communications
- Incentives and gamification
- Pilot programs
- Process improvement or other problem-solving teams

Systems
- Performance management
- Knowledge management

Your specific initiative is unique enough that we could not cover all the possible structural influence methods you might create in this workbook. Instead, in this section we will cover two structural influence methods that are crucial for all types of change:

Ensure Accountability
Change is impossible if people don't achieve goals and follow up on their commitments. We will start with project goals and measures, and then create accountability agreements for key individuals.

Pinpoint Communication
Haphazard messaging results in scattershot change. Good change communication consists of getting the appropriate message to the right people who then do something with it. In this chapter, we will generate a detailed communications plan.

In addition to applying the five levers of influence, structural influence methods are also useful ways to avoid or reduce resistance. Some provide information or build skills. Some motivate by connecting with values or adding a personal stake in the outcome. Others reduce fear by sharing control or making it easier to succeed. And others eliminate constraints by saving time and money.

Before we take on accountability and communication in detail, take a moment to specify the other structural influence methods you plan to implement to either move people in the direction of the future state or reduce the resistance you uncovered earlier in the workbook.

The five levers of influence and the ways to reduce resistance are two sides of the same coin. The five levers approach looks at the things we can add to influence change, while the resistance perspective looks at the things we want to avoid or fix. Both approaches can provide enlightenment that the other might not illuminate. So, we will look at structural influence both ways.

Remember the Force-Field Analysis from the Clarify The Change chapter? In the Uncover Resistance chapter, you essentially added to the right-hand side of the Force-Field Analysis in the Plan for Resistance Chart as the forces against change. Now, the Structural Influence Charts on the next pages help you fill in the left-hand side of the Force-Field Analysis, the forces towards change.

Forces Towards Change | **Forces Against Change**

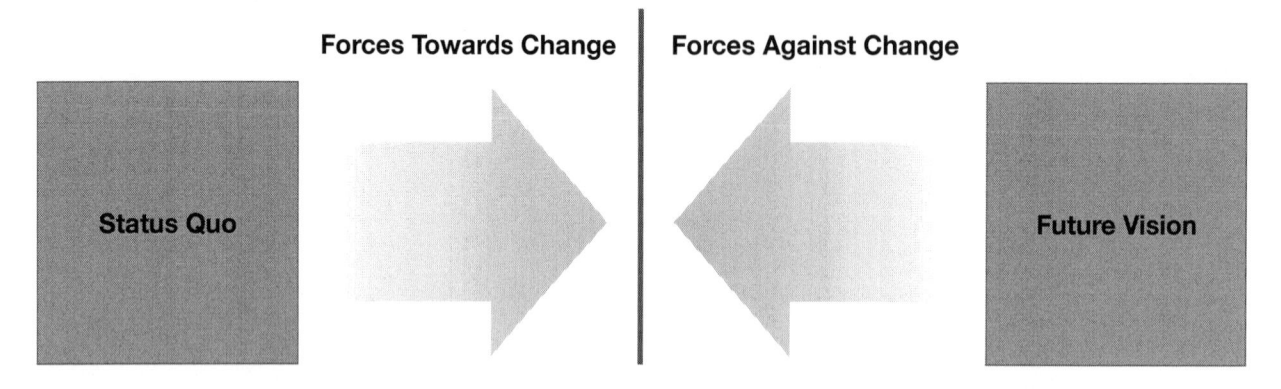

Status Quo → ← Future Vision

Force-Field Analysis

For each Stakeholder Group and Transition Theme, complete the Structural Influence Chart on the next page with the tools, programs, and systems you will implement to apply the five fundamental levers of influence. Review the Layers of Change Analysis and the Change Impact Assessment exercises, then consider those individuals and groups who will be moving through the transition. Next, identify some of the ways you can apply the levers of influence to help them move in the right direction.

On the second page, refer first to the Plan for Resistance Chart and the sources of resistance you identified for each Transition Theme. Then, identify the structural influence methods you can use to reduce each source of resistance.

Next, compare the two Structural Influence Charts. Together, they make up the Structural Influence methods you will design in more detail to accomplish the transitions and results you set out to achieve.

Structural Influence Chart - Fundamental Levers

Stakeholder Group:

From	Transition Theme	To

Source	Structural Influence Methods
Provide Clarity	
Enable Progress	
Build Trust	
Invite Participation	
Motivate Action	

Irresistible Change Guide © 2014 Enclaria LLC

Structural Influence Chart - Reduce Resistance

Stakeholder Group:

From	Transition Theme	To
	→	

Source	Structural Influence Methods
Valid Concerns	
Information	
Skills	
Motivation	
Power	
Fear	
Trust	
Resources	

© 2014 Enclaria LLC

Irresistible Change Guide

The Iterative Nature of Change

You may find that one or more structural influence methods you create is a transition unto itself. It is common for the means of change to be, in fact, a change. For example, starting a process improvement team as an influence method to encourage ownership of the improved process would itself be a transition for an organization that is not accustomed to working in process improvement teams.

These nested, overlapping transitions are part of what makes organizational change so complicated. The change itself is a change, and the things we create to help implement the end result are also changes. In fact, when you described the transitions earlier in this workbook, you may have already listed one or more structural influence methods as part of the change.

This workbook already provides the tools for you to work through each iteration as you design and discover them. When you identify additional transitions, go back to the Clarify the Change chapter and work through the Layers of Change Analysis for each. Then, fill in both sides of a new Force Field Analysis with the Plan for Resistance Chart and the Structural Influence Charts for those new transitions.

Ensure Accountability

Accountability Defined

Accountability is one of those principles of business that is an important foundation of organizational culture but is easily shrugged off as a buzzword. Ask someone in your organization to define accountability, and you may hear any number of answers, from "I don't know" to "following the rules" to "doing what you say you will do" to "disciplinary action." You might even see some eyes roll.

Accountability is rarely explicitly defined, whether for the organization as a whole, or for the departments and teams that work within them. While a well-designed performance management system may hint at the underlying accountability philosophy, rarely does an organization define the daily act of accountability, even for its leadership team for whom it is most important.

What is accountability? A quick search at Dictionary.com reveals the following definition: "ac·count·a·bil·i·ty [uh-koun-tuh-bil-i-tee]: the state of being accountable, liable, or answerable." Certainly, it is an obvious answer to the question, but it does not shed much light on what it means for people in organizations to be accountable.

Intuitively, everyone has a sense of what accountability means to them. A warehouse clerk is accountable for accurate parts inventory every month. A human resources director is accountable for ensuring the company heeds employment laws. A CEO is accountable for business results. For each of these examples, the word "accountable" could be replaced by "responsible." Each person is responsible for achieving a result.

Yet, accountability means more than responsibility. There is a sense that other people are involved. The same CEO is accountable to shareholders. The warehouse clerk is accountable to his manager. The human resources director is accountable to the employees. Accountability requires that someone has a stake in whether or not the desired result is achieved.

In fact, the person who is responsible for the result must also have a stake in achieving the outcome. There must be a consequence — positive or negative — based on whether or not the outcome is achieved.

The basic definition of accountability, then is: **Accountability is a promise to yourself and others to deliver specific, defined results, with consequences.**

How accountability is assigned and followed up in your organization defines how results-oriented your organization is. Explicitly defining accountability and setting clear guidelines for holding people accountable can go a long way towards achieving results.

At the end of this chapter we'll create accountability agreements that define accountability for key individuals in the organization. Before we look at individuals, we need to get more specific about what you plan to accomplish with this initiative, so we can create alignment.

Create a Project Scorecard

If you waited until the end of your change initiative before you looked to see if you made it to the intended destination, you would probably be disappointed. Although truthfully, you probably would never make it to the end because everyone would have given up on the project a long time ago without any evidence of improvement. To influence change, measure progress.

As a project manager, measure progress so you can see if what you are doing is working. That way, you can make adjustments as you go to help keep your initiative on track.

As a change agent, measure progress so you can help people see that their efforts are paying off. In the middle of a long change initiative, it might feel like nothing is happening despite a lot of work. It will help to have a way to say, "Look how far we've come!"

Use the scorecard template that follows to record the following components:

Date
Since some parts of the scorecard change over time, start with the current or effective date at the top of the page.

Objective
An objective is what you really want to happen as a result of the change initiative. Looking back at the Clarify the Change chapter, you can most likely find your objectives within the Before and After Chart. Each Transition Theme in the chart describes at least one objective. In the earlier ABC Corp example, the objectives might be "Build more innovative products" and "Take more informed risks."

The Balanced Scorecard methodology, a tool for measuring an organization's progress towards implementing its strategy developed by Robert Kaplan and David Norton, offers a good framework for selecting objectives. It offers four categories of objectives that you might consider for your project.

- *Financial*: Measure the dollars or other currency, or anything having to do with money.
- *Customer*: Determine success from the customer point of view (including internal customers).
- *Internal Process*: Show the mechanics of how you will achieve the initiative.
- *Organization*: Answer how the organization will support the initiative. This category includes things like leadership, teamwork, infrastructure, and organizational culture.

Having objectives in each of these areas gives you a complete and balanced look at what you are trying to accomplish.

Measure
The measure is what you are looking at to determine how well you are achieving your objective. The objective is usually something you can't inherently measure, so the measure is the proxy. For example, when you

measure employee turnover, your end goal is not to know how many people are leaving the company. You want to know how effective the company is at retaining talent. The turnover measure is just one way to estimate the objective of increasing employee satisfaction.

The alignment between objective and measure is a critical factor in the effectiveness of the measure. Good alignment means that when the measure moves in the direction you want, you are making progress toward your objective. Just because employee turnover decreases doesn't explicitly mean that satisfaction has gone up; it just means employees aren't leaving at the same rate as they were before. It is important to know the relationship between your measure and your objective.

When an objective and its measure are misaligned, one of two things happens. Either people will ignore it altogether because they see that there is no real connection, or you will end up with unintended consequences because people go after a measure that is unrelated to the objective. It is better to have a subjective measure that is aligned with its objective than to have a concrete measure that doesn't really tell you what you want to know.

Effective measures also have the following qualities:

- *Strategic*: Does the measure track progress toward achieving the objective?
- *Actionable*: Will you be able to do anything about it? Will it help you make decisions?
- *Operational*: Can you collect the data? Can people understand it and do they believe it?
- *Economical*: Is the cost of collecting the information feasible?

Frequency

The frequency is a single word that describes how often you will take and report the measurement.

How often should you measure progress? Every year, quarter, month, week, day…? The answer depends on what you are measuring. You don't want the time between measurements to be so short that you won't see progress in between because nothing moved. At the same time, you also don't want to wait so long that you'll find out too late that you should have made an adjustment sooner. Find a frequency that will show concrete progress and also provide timely information for making decisions.

Common frequencies:

Once	Annual	Semi-Annual
Quarterly	Bi-Monthly	Monthly
Weekly	Daily	Ongoing

Target & Due Date

The target is the value of the measure you want to achieve by the target due date. If the measure is quantifiable, the target will be a number. If qualitative, use words to describe the target.

Current Status

The current status is the current value of the measure. The number or description should be the same format as the target for easy comparison.

Owner

The owner is the primary person responsible and accountable for achieving the target.

Source

The source is the primary person responsible for collecting the data, conducting analysis and tracking the measure. The source may be the same or different from the owner, depending on who has ready access to the information.

Complete the Initiative Scorecard on the following page for your project. To foster commitment, invite others, especially those who will be objective owners, to contribute to developing the scorecard.

Initiative Scorecard

Date:

Objective	Measure	Frequency	Target & Due Date	Current Status	Owner	Source

Make Measures Work

It's been said, "What gets measured gets done." Taken at face value, the statement means that if you want something done, then simply measure it. Anyone who has tried to implement a scorecard or performance dashboard knows that just because you measure something doesn't mean it's automatically going to change. There are a number of caveats and prerequisites to the well-worn platitude. The following are a couple ways to make measures work.

Focus on action

A measure tells you whether an objective needs attention and what its priority is. It will rarely tell you what action to take; it will only tell you that action should be taken. Still, many teams get bogged down in the accuracy and derivation of the measure itself instead of taking action with the information that they do have.

Focus on the initiatives that will move the dial even if you don't yet know exactly where the dial is located. As better information becomes available, you can adjust your report to show what is truly happening. If better information is too difficult to collect, decide what is good enough or get a new measure. A team that only talks about measures without taking action toward objectives is a team that will quickly lose interest in measurement and will only tread water on what really matters: real change.

Make reports meaningful

The detailed 1-2 page scorecard with rows of measures provides a great summary, however, it does not impart as much information as detailed, visual measure reports. At the risk of using more paper, ink and time, provide people with an interesting graphic that tells a story and helps them make decisions. Best practice measure reports, like the example on the next page, include the scorecard details, plus the following additional information, on one page per measure:

- *Chart*: Instead of showing a static number like on the scorecard, the chart shows the measure's progress over time, so you can see if you are moving in the right direction. The target is featured, to compare with the actual measure. An arrow indicates which direction you want the number to move on the chart.
- *Status Indicator*: The indicator is a quick visual cue that shows how well the project is accomplishing each objective. Examples are red/yellow/green indicators, where green means all is well, yellow means it needs attention, and red means it needs urgent attention; smiley and frown faces; or thumbs up and thumbs down. Also listed are the assessment criteria for determining the indicator.
- *What are we measuring*: A brief explanation of what is being measured and where it comes from.
- *Why is it important*: The link between the measure and the objective.
- *What does our performance tell us*: An interpretation of what the current status indicates is happening.
- *What is being done*: The current status of initiatives underway or planned to make progress.

Great measure reports make it easy for people to quickly understand what is going on. Instead of having meetings that spend time explaining the measure and its status, focus meetings on making decisions about what should be done to achieve the objective.

Scorecard Report Template

Sample Measure Name

Objective: The measure on this page shows you how well you are achieving this objective.

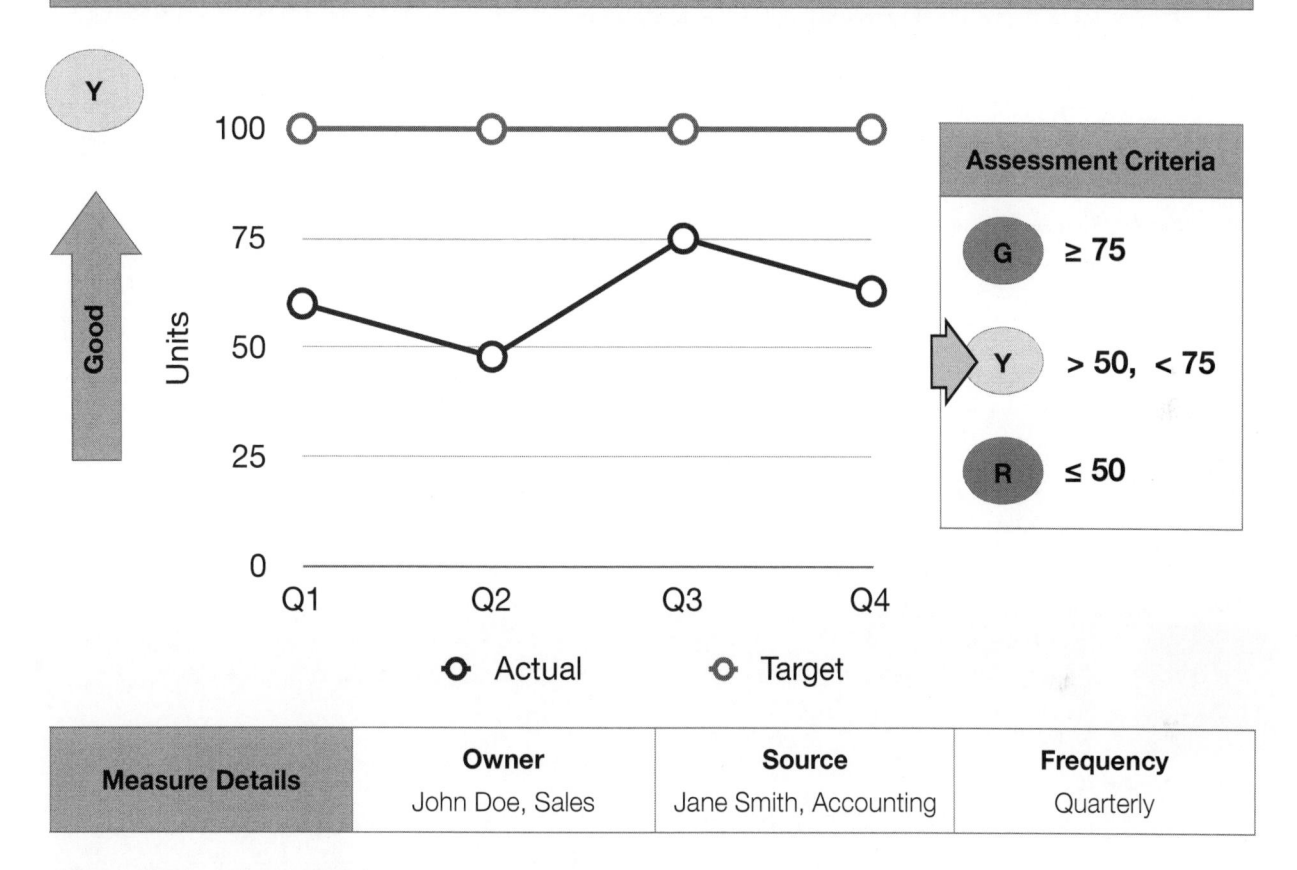

Y

100 —————————————————

Good ↑ Units

75

50

25

0
  Q1   Q2   Q3   Q4

○ Actual   ○ Target

Assessment Criteria

G ≥ 75

Y > 50, < 75

R ≤ 50

Measure Details	Owner John Doe, Sales	Source Jane Smith, Accounting	Frequency Quarterly

What are we measuring?
Describe what the measure is. Explain the data source and how the measure is calculated.

Why is it important?
Explain how the measure is linked to the objective.

What does our performance tell us?
Provide an interpretation of what the current status indicates is happening. Share what is working and what isn't, plus what is impacting the performance.

What are we doing about it?
Detail the projects that are underway or planned to improve or maintain the status.

Irresistible Change Guide © 2014 Enclaria LLC

Create Accountability Agreements

In this chapter, we have defined specific objectives for your initiative and attached owners to them. In previous chapters, we have identified relationships and expectations for key leaders of the initiative. Now it's time to combine these pieces to create accountability agreements for individuals.

The purpose of the accountability agreement is not to create a "gotcha" scenario, where people are reprimanded or punished for slipping from a contract. On the contrary, the agreement is designed to both set clear expectations and to gain commitment to the initiative. Commitment means people pledge to do their part to implement change. It is much more than simply head-nodding. Those who are committed to change complete tasks, strive to achieve goals and align their words with their actions. By coming to an agreement with other parties, everyone knows what to expect and can stay on the same page by working together properly from the beginning.

Behavioral research shows that if people commit, verbally or in writing, to an idea or goal, they are more likely to honor that commitment. The desire to not contradict oneself is so strong that even if the original incentive or motivation is removed after they have already agreed, people tend to continue to honor the agreement. The accountability agreement takes advantage of the natural human need to heed commitments.

The accountability agreement is a one-page document that consolidates the objectives each person commits to achieving, the measures he will track, the roles and relationships he will uphold, and the consequences of the actual results.

The process for assigning accountability asks four questions. Answer the questions within the following guidelines.

Accountable for what?
Accountability starts with an outcome, a result that needs to be accomplished. It is important to distinguish between responsibility for activities and accountability for results. Micro-managers define the activities that are expected and then hold employees responsible for performing those activities. However, accountability for results requires room for judgment and decision-making. Someone can't be accountable for an end result if someone else tells him what to do and how to do it. Ultimately, it is the end result that forms the expectation upon which accountability is based.

Who is accountable?
Next, assign who holds the responsibility for the result. Ultimately, accountability is not shared, although responsibility may be. A manager who has taken on responsibility for a result may delegate that responsibility to an employee; however, the manager does not give up the accountability for that result, nor does he truly share the accountability with that employee, since they are accountable to different people.

Accountable to whom?
Everyone is accountable first to himself. The result must be achieved within the scope of one's own personal values, ethics and abilities. Identify the party or parties who have a stake in the outcome. For example, who will receive status reports and updates throughout the project? If there is more than one stakeholder,

determine if the expected outcomes are the same. If the expectations are different, then an agreement should be made between the stakeholders on how those outcomes are related.

What are the consequences?

Accountability is meaningless without consequences, positive or negative. Consequences are the expected outcomes, or what will happen as a result of the commitment being achieved or not. The outcomes may comprise the effect on the organization, on customers or other outside stakeholders, or the person making the commitment. Consequences also include the rewards or repercussions enforced by others, artificially added to the natural consequences in order to increase motivation.

The concept of holding someone accountable comes in here. If someone accomplishes the results they promised to achieve, then he should be recognized for that. If someone misses his target, then he should at best not receive the recognition, and at worst he should be penalized. It is important to define the consequence up front.

Accountability is not conditional. Accepting unconditional responsibility means there are no excuses and no one to blame, even if events are beyond one's control. Also, accountability for results means activities are not enough. It is not enough to execute activities perfectly if the desired outcome is not achieved. If people receive the expected reward for trying hard, then accountability will not work. If the organization wants to reward risk-taking or trying hard, then it should be done outside of the original accountability agreement for results.

The template for the Accountability Agreement is on the next page. For each individual who is accountable for a piece of the initiative, create an agreement that includes the following:

Achievement of Targets

Under "I am responsible for and commit to achieving the following," list the objectives that this individual is responsible for achieving.

Roles and Relationships

Under "I will provide my support by fulfilling my role in relationship to these parties," detail the roles this individual will fulfill for key individuals or groups. From your work in the Leadership section of the workbook, list the processes, behaviors and mindsets they will exhibit to support change.

Outcomes

Under "I recognize the following outcomes of my efforts," identify the positive results of his follow-through, and the negative consequences of lack of follow-through.

Complete the Accountability Agreement on the next page with each individual that you would like to demonstrate commitment to supporting the initiative. Accountability is something that must be owned by the person accountable, not imposed by others, to ensure true commitment. Invite each person to complete the form and then start a conversation to agree on the details. Invite them to sign and date the agreement to solidify their commitment.

Accountability Agreement

Name:

I am responsible for and commit to achieving the following:			
Objective	Measure	Target	Due Date

I will provide my support by fulfilling my role in relationship to these parties:	
Group or Individual	My Role

I recognize the following outcomes of my efforts:	
Results - If I Do	Consequences - If I Don't

Name   Date

104   © 2014 Enclaria LLC   Irresistible Change Guide

Resistance to Accountability

Accountability, as an influence tool, combats resistance in a few ways. First, the objectives and targets set clear expectations for results, filling an information gap. Second, the challenge of accomplishing meaningful goals, along with the expectation of consequences, provides motivation. And third, following through on the accountability agreements builds trust and credibility.

At the same time, like other structural influence methods, for some organizations, fostering accountability is itself a transition, complete with its own resistance against it. While I encourage you to complete your own Plan for Resistance for implementing accountability, if you experience or expect resistance, these are common sources:

- People may have valid concerns that the targets that have been set are not realistic, in which case they are not motivating. They may not share this concern because they do not want to appear incapable or unwilling.
- A shift from being rewarded for working hard to being expected to achieve results may drive a fear from loss of control. It is easier to control one's own behavior than results, which are often affected by factors outside one's control.
- Adding responsibility for tracking measures may generate resistance when it is a strain on resources. Take into consideration the value of having the information versus the cost of collecting it when deciding which measures to track.

Since we are talking about individual accountability, usually within a group, the recommended approach is to complete the Individual Resistance Assessment when you experience resistance. Then, openly work through the resistance by Starting Conversations with individuals or Facilitating Meetings to discuss accountability within a group, two tools we will explore in the Personal Influence section later in this workbook.

Pinpoint Communication

The Challenge of Communicating Change

No change initiative can occur successfully without proper organizational communication. In organizational communication, as opposed to personal communication, messages are conveyed to audiences with the purposes of keeping people informed and mobilizing the organization for change. Communication is the means to gain attention, educate, and get individuals and groups to take action to move the change initiative forward.

As an internal change agent for your organization, communication is one of the main tools you use to reach your goal and desired outcome. Yet, frequently those who are responsible for implementing change use communication in a haphazard fashion, without a solid plan. The resulting hodgepodge of newsletters, posters and meetings tells a less-than-compelling story of change.

By the end of this chapter, you will have developed a detailed plan for communicating your change initiative, focused on getting a consistent and concise message to the right people using effective channels at the appropriate time. The act of developing the plan itself is not complicated. However, there are a number of challenges inherent to change communication that you will need to overcome along the way. Among them are:

- Ensuring consistency between media and messengers
- Overcoming the rapidly increasing amount of information that distracts employees from your message
- Communicating enough, in quantity and content, to impart the message effectively
- Involving the audience in the communication, instead of just telling.

This chapter aims to help you overcome these challenges by incorporating them into the structure of the questions and exercises as you develop your change communication plan.

This chapter is a place to organize your thoughts and generate a plan for how to gain attention, educate, and engage the members of your organization in your change initiative. First, we will identify the intended audience of communication, and determine what your message will be. Next, we will map out how the communication will occur, including the media you will use, who the messenger will be, and how often it will happen.

Target Your Audience

Your change initiative is not one-size-fits-all. The expectations of different groups vary when it comes to the new behaviors and mindsets that are required for success. How you communicate to each group should vary accordingly. In this section, you will identify your various audiences, so you can target communication to them with laser focus.

How you divide your organization into different audiences will drive the content, style and tone for each message. Most likely, your audience segments will mirror the Stakeholder and Employee groups you identified in earlier chapters, although you may want to combine or divide groups for the purposes of communication. Like the Stakeholder and Employee groups, you may segment your audience into groups such as:

Organization Level
Split the organization by title: executives, upper-management, middle-management, supervisors, front-line employees.

Departments, Functional Areas or Business Units
Group people by the task they have in relation to your initiative, or by natural organizational boundaries.

Regional or Geography
Divide the organization by regions or languages.

Union or Non-Union
Split employees between those in a bargaining unit and those that are not.

External Stakeholders
Consider groups that are not a part of the organization, such as the media, the public, regulators and the community.

Answer the questions on the next page to help identify your various audience groups:

Target Audiences

What are the natural audience groups within your organization?

Based on your initiative, what groups are the focus of the change?

What groups may need special messaging (terminology, culture, language)?

What groups or individuals may have a unique impact on the success of your initiative?

Craft Your Message

The content of your communication is the message you will deliver to the organization. Organizational communication is made up of broad-based themes that help ensure consistency while maintaining flexibility to customize for each audience.

In this section, you will learn about the three main purposes of change communication. Then, we will develop messages to deliver to your organization that serve each purpose.

The Three E's of Change Messages

Ultimately, the goal to any communication program is to have the audience do something with the information. To that end, there are three purposes to any communication plan:

Entice

For one, you want to gain attention by making your message stand out from the countless other inputs that employees deal with every day. With all the distractions employees face, it can be difficult to break through. The key to gaining attention is to pique the audience's curiosity, to make the message stand out, and to give them a reason to learn more.

- What's in it for me?
- Why should I care?
- What is my part in this?

Educate

Once you have the attention of your audience, the next step is to inform and educate them about your initiative. It's time to share what they need to know.

- What do I need to know?
- What should I be aware of?
- What information will help me succeed?

Engage

The next step is to motivate the audience to take action with the information they have been given. Invite them to participate, let them know what needs to be done, and share expectations. Since the ultimate goal is to have people do something with the information you provide, enlist them into the initiative and motivate them to participate.

- What should I do?
- How do I get involved?

On the Customize Your Message chart on the next page, list each of the key audience groups in the left-hand column. Then, brainstorm the high-level concepts you want to communicate with each. We will add further detail on specific messages in the next section. Start with the overarching, organization-wide message.

Customize Your Message

Audience	Entice Why should I care?	Educate What should I know?	Engage What should I do?

Refine the Message

Now that you have identified the general message you would like to impart to each audience, let's take a look at specific types of messages you can use to convey that information.

The following are some of the messages you might choose to communicate about change, along with the purpose each generally serves:

Entice Why should I care?	Educate What should I know?	Engage What should I do?
Urgency Vision Change Narrative Recognition Awards & Celebrations Encouragement	Strategy Progress Updates Reminders Announcements	Cases & Examples Invitations Instructions Priorities Goals & Deadlines Expectations Feedback

Messages to Communicate Change

Urgency

The reason for moving away from the status quo, the sense of urgency was developed in the Assess Reality chapter. Urgency makes the audience uncomfortable with the current state of affairs. It provides the impetus to change in the first place.

Vision

As we developed in the Define the Future chapter, your vision is a picture of the future. It provides a clear view of the common destination for the audience. The vision fosters hope, inspires the audience, and helps them prepare for what's next.

Change Narrative

The change narrative is the story of the initiative. It brings the change to life by making those going through the change the central characters of a compelling epic. They become heroes that join together to defeat a common enemy.

Recognition

Acknowledge the work and accomplishments of those who are helping the change move forward. Recognize when people are doing the key behaviors and processes that are expected. Those who receive recognition will be inspired to continue, and the audience may be motivated to earn it themselves.

Awards & Celebrations

More formal than recognition, awards and celebrations are special occasions for acknowledging good work and progress towards change. Plan ahead for what you want to celebrate, so you can make sure it happens.

Encouragement
Encouragement shows the audience that the messenger believes they can accomplish the feat that is in front of them. It bolsters confidence, reassures the audience that everything will be okay, and lets them know they will be supported along the way.

Strategy
The strategy is the game plan for how the audience will achieve the vision. It comprises the high-level objectives that, when they accomplish them, will achieve the desired outcomes of the initiative.

Progress Updates
Just as you want to measure progress to see how well the project is going, you want to share that progress with the audience. Progress updates impart a sense of accomplishment for those involved and build momentum for those who are watching to see if it will work.

Reminders
Once the initiative starts rolling, sometimes the audience will need reminders to keep going. Different from a repeat of the same message, a reminder prompts the audience to do something they have already agreed to do.

Announcements
Announcements are usually one-time messages (although it could be a series) that declare something new is happening. They are used to gain attention and impart news.

Cases & Examples
Real-life examples are a great way to demonstrate what is expected of the audience. At first, the cases may be from outside the organization, and once the project gets going, they can come from inside so the audience can see their peers succeeding at implementing the change.

Invitations
An invitation extends an opportunity to the audience to participate in the change. Whether it is to join a team, enter a contest, or submit ideas, inviting the audience asks them to take part. The more personal the invitation, the more compelling it will be at the individual level.

Instructions
Instructions provide a detailed step-by-step guide for how to do something. When it comes to change, instructions may detail a new or improved process, or they may explain how to participate in a structural influence program, for example.

Priorities
Priorities communicate to the audience what is important — especially with respect to other things. Priorities demonstrate values and help people decide how to allocate their resources and attention.

Goals & Deadlines

From the Ensure Accountability chapter, goals are defined as the combination of the initiative's objectives, measures and targets. Sharing the goals and their respective deadlines with the audience ensures that everyone is aiming for the same targets along the same timeline.

Expectations

Sharing desired outcomes, processes, behaviors and mindsets helps ensure there is no confusion about what is expected. For example, based on the Gain Leadership Support chapter, you might expect a leadership audience to model key behaviors, express certain messages, and reinforce those behaviors in others.

Feedback

As the audience incorporates the change into their routines, let them know what they are doing well and what needs improvement as they go. Also, enable the audience to provide you with feedback about how the change is going from their perspective.

Communication for change should not be developed centrally in a vacuum. When it comes to designing the actual messages, invite others to participate. Then, you can distribute the collaborative messages to the rest of the audiences to extend the conversation.

Develop Message Plans

On the next page, complete the Message Plan for each audience. Start with the broader audiences, and then complete the plan for more focused audiences.

At the top, start by reiterating the high-level messages of change for that audience, from the Customize Your Message table.

Next, in the Purpose column, write the main purpose of the message: Entice, Educate, or Engage. Most likely, you will start with Entice, since you need to gain attention and share purpose before conveying what people need to know and what they need to do. In the Message column, list the message (for example, vision, updates, recognition, etc.) that you will share with the audience. Add your own detail to make the message specific to your initiative and audience.

Then, choose your timeline by marking a start date for that message, an end date, and the frequency with which you will convey that message in between. The following are common frequencies:

Once	Annual	Semi-Annual
Quarterly	Bi-Monthly	Monthly
Weekly	Ongoing	Anniversary

We will explore how to get your message to the audience in the next section. For now, decide when and how often each audience should receive each message. Then, you can determine which mix of media will best work to get your messages across.

Message Plan by Audience

Audience	Entice Why should I care?	Educate What should I know?	Engage What should I do?

Purpose	Message	Start Date	Frequency	End Date

Select Your Media

Now that you know what you would like to communicate, it is time to determine the means of communication. In this section, you will evaluate the effectiveness of various communication vehicles in your organization. Then, you will select the messenger and the frequency of each message.

The means of communication are continually changing with the advances of technology, but today they include the following general categories and examples.

- *In-Person*: Meetings, one-on-one conversations, presentations, speeches…
- *Audio/Visual*: Voice mail, podcasts, videos, teleconferences…
- *Written*: Newsletters, memos, posters, tchotchkes, email…
- *Internet*: Website, blogs, micro-blogging (Twitter, Yammer), discussion groups, webinars…

Before we decide which of these means of communication, or vehicles, will convey your messages to the appropriate audience, let's evaluate the effectiveness of various communication vehicles.

Cost
What is the cost of the vehicle in terms of time and money? Usually, the communication vehicles with the most impact, like in-person meetings, have the highest cost. Also, vehicles that are new to your organization may cost more than those that already exist.

Trust / Credibility
How likely is the audience to believe the information communicated through this vehicle? The closest relationships generally have more trust.

Access
Which of your audiences have access to this vehicle? Which vehicles have limited access? Electronic vehicles are limited to those with computer access. In-person meetings work best for those who are geographically close.

Focus
How much information will you be able to convey effectively using this vehicle, and what type of information is typically conveyed? For example, a video shares more information than an email, which in turn shares more than a poster.

Frequency
How often can this method be reasonably used? What is the minimum interval between events? A town hall meeting will probably not happen every day, whereas a blog might.

Use the Vehicle Effectiveness Table on the next page to assess how each of the following vehicles measures against these criteria in your organization. Identify additional vehicles that you may use that are not listed, and insert them into the blank rows provided.

Vehicle Effectiveness Table

Vehicle	Cost	Trust	Access	Focus	Frequency
Measure:	Time, Resources	High/Med/Low	Universal/Limited	Type of Info	Minimum Interval
1-1 Meeting					
Small Group					
Town Hall					
Podcast					
Video					
Teleconference					
Newsletter					
Memo					
Poster					
E-mail					
Website					
Blog					
Microblog					
Online Group					
Webinar					

Choose the Messenger

The messenger is the voice of the communication. It is the person who delivers the message. For example, is it an email from the CEO, a one-on-one conversation with a supervisor, or an article written by you?

It may be tempting to believe that as the change agent you are the best messenger. After all, it is difficult to control the words that come out of someone else's mouth. However, if the organization is to believe that the leadership team is committed to the project, it might be best for the message to come from them. Plus, the closer the messenger is to the audience (for example, a direct supervisor), the more the audience will relate to and trust the message.

Select Vehicle Frequency

How often the message is delivered will depend on a number of variables:

- The cost of the vehicle
- The nature of the vehicle (posters are ongoing, an annual report is annual)
- The availability of information and timing of updates
- The consumption capacity of the audience

Map Out Your Communication Plan

Now it's time to put all this information together to map out your change communication plan, starting on the next page. Complete one Communication Plan by Audience/Message for each audience. Start with the most general audience, such as the entire organization, and then focus on smaller groups with focused messages.

Using a calendar, fill in the dates across the top. Depending on how specific you want to make your plan, you may choose to organize your plan by months, weeks, or days.

Using the Message Plan by Audience, list the messages down the left-hand column. Based on the start and end dates and the frequency, mark with a check which dates each message will be conveyed to that audience.

Next, at the bottom of the table, select which vehicle and messenger will best convey those messages to your audience within that timeframe. If it makes sense to have more than one vehicle in that timeframe, then skip this step and continue with the Communication Plan by Vehicle/Messenger to organize your plan.

On the next page, we will take the Plan by Audience/Message and transform it into a Plan by Vehicle/Messenger so you can better manage the individual pieces of media. Note: The Plan by Vehicle/Messenger is a place to compile your messages for *all* audiences.

Transfer the dates from the Audience/Message Plan to the left-hand column. Select the audience and message combinations that will be communicated via one vehicle in that timeframe. Then, write the combinations in one row each.

Next, list the appropriate Vehicle/Messenger pairing for each Audience/Message combination.

Then, you will have a Communication Plan for your initiative!

Communication Plan by Audience/Message

Audience:

Date: Message													
Vehicle													
Messenger													

Communication Plan by Vehicle/Messenger

Date	Vehicle	Messenger	Audience(s)	Message(s)

Evaluating Your Plan
Now that you have laid out your communication plan, check it for the following:

Resources
Verify that your messengers are not overwhelmed with communications duties. Check that your audiences are not being bombarded with messages.

Sequence
One audience group may need to receive the message before another group, such as those who are responsible to pass along the message to or answer questions for another audience. Also, check that the general sequence of messages makes sense for the roll out of your initiative.

Focus
Review your individual vehicles to make sure you don't communicate too many things in any one vehicle. You may need to use multiple vehicles to convey all the messages, or stagger the timing to maintain the focus of each vehicle.

Monitor Your Organization's Nonverbal Communication
It is widely cited that verbal communication makes up only 7% of a total message during a conversation. That is, 93% percent of the meaning within the conversation comes from outside the words that we use. These nonverbal aspects of communication include gestures, posture, intonation, and facial expressions. It turns out the concrete language is by far the least important factor in our interpretation and understanding of what the other person saying.

A similar phenomenon happens in organizations. Consider that the equivalent to verbal communication in organizations are the formal words that come to employees in the form of official documents: values and mission statements, strategy, policies, newsletters, websites, announcements, press releases, and other communication devices. The rest of internal communication comes from everything else employees experience. Similar to a conversation, the vast majority of meaning and understanding is generated by "nonverbal" communication.

The following are examples of "nonverbal" communication in organizations that speaks louder than words:

Accountability
Employees assess which policies count and which ones are merely guidelines based on how consistently they are enforced. Processes and procedures are generally followed to the extent that they are required.

"Everyone must contact the IT help desk to resolve computer issues"
(unless you know who to call to avoid waiting).

Rewards
Rewards in all their forms tell employees how to be successful. Traditional incentive programs signal expectations but may conflict with stated values or even inadvertently motivate a different behavior than what

is desired. Furthermore, who gets promoted and what behaviors elicit praise send powerful messages about what is expected.

"Safety first!"
(but here's your efficiency bonus.)

Decisions

How managers spend resources speaks volumes about what they truly value and prioritize. The decisions they make about how to allocate funds and how they spend their own time demonstrates what they believe will lead to success.

"Strategic initiatives are important"
(until we need to cut something out of the budget).

Management behavior

More than anything, employees look at the behavior modeled by management to see if it matches what is officially communicated. The most influential person in this regard is an employee's own boss. The attitudes and behaviors displayed by people in authority tell the real story of what is expected.

"We value employees' ideas"
(but not the terrible one you just shared).

Employees will rely on "nonverbal" communication to understand what is expected and to decide appropriate action in the midst of uncertainty. When introduced to news of change, many employees will take the stance, "I'll believe it when I see it." It is not enough for them to hear it or read it. It is imperative to monitor your organization's "nonverbal" communication to ensure that actions and behaviors are consistent with your official change message.

Personal Influence

Personal Influence

The True Power of the Change Agent

When I coach clients one-on-one, we often work through clarifying the change, understanding the role leaders should play, and designing structural influence methods. But, of the four drivers of change, personal influence is where we spend the most time and effort. You can plan and design as much as you can, but until you personally take action to make things happen, the initiative will not gain the traction required to make progress.

To use this workbook effectively, you will have to take what we have talked about so far and use it outside of these pages. For example, you may need to:

- Invite people to participate in assessing the current reality and defining the future.
- Work with leaders to identify transitions and explore the four layers of each.
- Have conversations to uncover resistance and gain support.
- Convince leaders of their unique role in change and provide feedback when they don't fulfill it.
- Get people to use the tools, programs, and systems designed to add structural influence.
- Follow up and hold people accountable to finishing tasks and achieving goals.
- Help communication messengers stay aligned with the message.

All of these examples require the secret sauce that only you can provide as a change agent. You bridge the gap between the design and implementation with personal influence.

When figuring out how to personally influence change, my clients and I typically work on three approaches. We spend time preparing for conversations to influence individuals. We work on how to design and facilitate meetings to influence a group. And, we find ways to increase their personal power within the organization so they have the desired impact.

In this section, we will cover the following ways you can best improve and leverage your influence.

Boost Your Power
Power is your ability to get things done in your organization. First, we will start by looking at your sources of power in the organization. Using the Personal Power Inventory, we will discover the opportunities for you to gain more influence.

Start Conversations

Organizational change ultimately happens at an individual level. Much of the resistance you encounter can only be dealt with through one-on-one conversations. The willingness to start, and the ability to hold, difficult conversations set great change agents apart from those who get stuck. This chapter will provide tips for effective conversations as well as tools to prepare for them.

Facilitate Meetings

Change requires a lot of meetings in order to get people together and make coordinated progress. Whether you are running the meeting or acting as a participant, assume the role of facilitator to ensure time is used effectively, progress is made, and issues are dealt with. In this chapter, we will explore the different types of meetings and how to prepare for each type for maximum effectiveness.

Before we explore these personal influence approaches in detail, let's identify the gaps left to fill in our model. Just like with the Structural Influence section, we will add new forces towards change to help you make progress towards the Future Vision. The Personal Influence Charts on the next two pages help you complete the left-hand side of the Force-Field Analysis, this time with things you or your team will personally do to influence change.

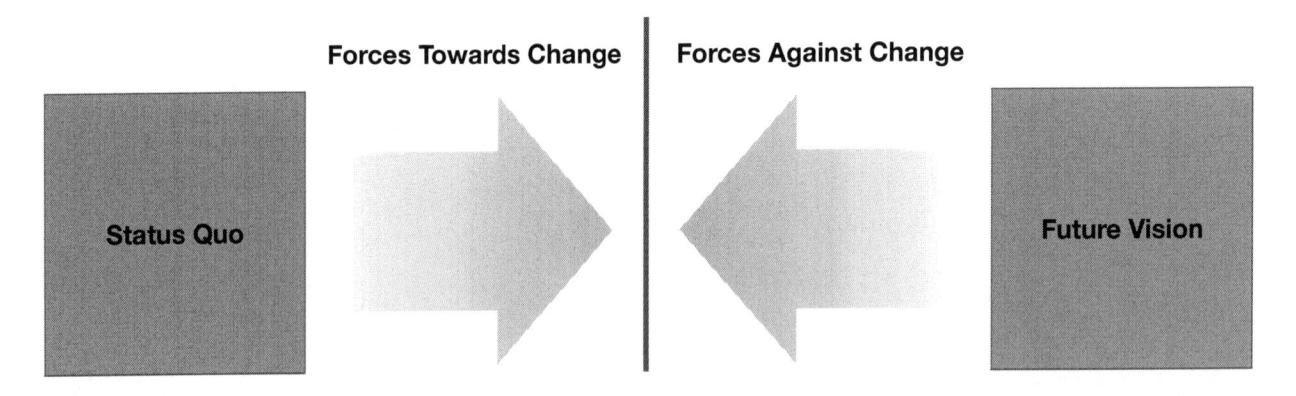

Force-Field Analysis

For each Transition Theme and Stakeholder Group (or individual), complete the Personal Influence Chart on the next page by identifying ways you can personally apply the five fundamental levers of influence. On the second page, list the conversations, meetings, and other ways you will personally work to reduce the sources of resistance you identified for the same Transition Theme.

Personal Influence Chart - Fundamental Levers

Stakeholder Group/Individual:

From	Transition Theme	To

Source	Personal Influence Methods
Provide Clarity	
Enable Progress	
Build Trust	
Invite Participation	
Motivate Action	

Irresistible Change Guide © 2014 Enclaria LLC

Personal Influence Chart - Reduce Resistance

Stakeholder Group/Individual:

From	Transition Theme	To

Source	Personal Influence Opportunities
Valid Concerns	
Information	
Skills	
Motivation	
Power	
Fear	
Trust	
Resources	

The Glue That Holds It Together

Change agents use common metaphors for how they feel while implementing change. Pushing a boulder uphill. Swimming upstream. Banging my head against a wall. The glue that holds it all together. All of these depictions describe the feeling that if you were removed from the situation, everything would snap back to the status quo immediately. I think the inherent frustration in this point of view comes from the expectation that, like in the movie *Field of Dreams*, "If you build it, they will come." The truth is, if change were that easy, they wouldn't need you there to implement it!

I would like to offer an alternate expectation that personal influence is a vital part of change, and as a change agent you should relish the chance to hone and use it when the opportunity presents itself. And it will; the need for personal influence is continual throughout the change process, from the first discussions until you can finally let go because the change is the new status quo.

Change is not linear, and the need for personal influence pops up throughout the process. Therefore, I expect that you would come back to these chapters often, to evaluate your personal influence in specific situations and to prepare for critical conversations and meetings as necessary.

All the techniques you can use to influence are too numerous to detail in these chapters. However, I would like to point you to another resource, the book I published in 2010 called *99 Ways to Influence Change*. Most of the *99 Ways* are personal influence methods you can use within the context of your conversations and meetings. In the appendix of this workbook, I have included two lists of the *99 Ways*, one categorized by which fundamental lever of influence they apply, and another sorted by which source of resistance they are most likely to reduce. If you would like more detail, the book is available at www.enclaria.com/influencechangebook.

Boost Your Power

Sources of Personal Power in Organizations

To be an effective change agent, you must have some power within your organization. In general, power is the energy to make something happen. In the context of an organization, your personal power directly impacts your ability to influence change. Without it, you're just spinning your wheels.

Having power provides benefits that help you implement change. For example, the more power you have, the more freedom you are given to take action without permission. Power enables you to make decisions, especially those that affect other people. Since people tend to pay more attention to those who have power, with it you can be more effective at modeling behavior and having your message and ideas heard.

So then, where does power come from? In an organization, your ability to make things happen depends on others' willingness to let you. They choose — consciously or not — to pay attention to you, to allow you to influence them, to accept your decisions, and to move in the direction you suggest. Power is not, then, something you can create independently for yourself. Power is given to you by other people.

It may seem pointless to try to increase your personal power if you have to rely on other people to give it to you. Fortunately, there are sources of power you can draw upon that are within your control. As you grow in these four areas, you will be given more power in your organization.

Authority

When we think of who has power in organizations, we automatically think of those whose positions give them authority. Based on tradition, management titles — officers, vice presidents, directors, managers, supervisors — indicate a hierarchy so we know who has more or less power than we do. Titles are shortcuts to communicating status. They tell us who is in charge of something, and who is the boss.

But, authority is more than just a title. Having authority means you are responsible and accountable for achieving something, with the freedom to accomplish it. Authority comes with resources (even if it's your own time) and the ability to decide how they will be used. Authority can be delegated by others who already have some. In fact, when you are truly given authority, we say you are "empowered."

Knowledge, Skills and Expertise

You have probably heard the saying, "Knowledge is power." There are a number of ways in which this statement is true in organizations. When you have knowledge, people seek you out for your opinion. They listen to you, and often defer to you as the expert. Applying your knowledge and skills also helps you succeed, which increases your chances of gaining authority. And, sharing your expertise elicits feelings of respect and reciprocity in your relationships.

For your knowledge to translate to power, it must be relevant to the success of the organization, and you need to know at least as much as the people around you, and probably more. As a change agent, you should be knowledgeable about the change you are delivering, and you must also be the subject matter expert about change itself.

Relationships

You also gain power in organizations through your relationships. You have greater power from the people you frequently interact with, due in part to proximity; you are around certain people more, so you have more opportunities to influence them. More importantly, your closest relationships benefit from greater trust. The more people trust you, the more power they are willing to give you.

Your span of power within your organization depends on who you know. Your relationships with those who have authority increase your own power, because they can now use their power on your behalf. Your relationships with the people who are going through the change are important, since people are influenced by people they like. As you expand your network of relationships, your power will grow, not just because there are more people to give you power, but also because there are more sources of knowledge and authority for you to draw upon when you need them.

Confidence and Courage

While power is ultimately something that is given to you by other people, you are the one who chooses to use the power you have been given. Yes, you already have power in the form of your existing authority, knowledge, and relationships — and you can earn more by exercising what you have and using it effectively. You need both the confidence to know that you have power, and the courage to use it.

Your personal power is worthless unless you use it. Acknowledge the power that you have. Be willing to do and say what needs to be done and said. If you need something, then ask for it. No one else can use your personal power for you. If you don't use it, it is a wasted resource.

Identify Your Sources of Power

Now that we know where personal power comes from in organizations, let's take a look at your sources of power. Complete the Personal Power Inventory that starts on the next page to identify where you currently get your power from, and discover where you might find more.

Personal Power Inventory

Place a check mark next to the statements that are true for you and this change initiative. Then count the check marks and divide by the total number of statements to get a percent score for each source.

✓	Authority
	I have a title that clearly indicates my level of authority within the organization.
	I am accountable for achieving the goals of this initiative.
	I have the freedom to get things done the way that I want.
	I make decisions that impact the initiative.
	I control my own time at work.
	I manage a budget or other funds for the organization.
	Others come to me to act on their behalf.
	People identify me as the leader of the project.
	I hold others accountable for doing what they say they will do.
	People look to me to know what to do next.
	Total Count for Authority

✓	Expertise
	I have prior experience working on a similar project.
	I contribute knowledge that helps others make decisions.
	I am considered by others as an expert in this area.
	Others come to me seeking advice, opinions, or answers.
	I conduct training for this initiative.
	I continue to learn more about related topics.
	I have a degree or certification that designates my competence in this area.
	I actively participate in professional organizations that specialize in relevant topics.
	Total Count for Expertise

✓	**Relationships**
	People involved in this project know my name.
	I work in close proximity with the people working on this project.
	I am able to get an audience with people who have more authority than me.
	I have a direct connection with those I need to influence.
	I have a good relationship with my boss.
	I have a reputation for being trustworthy.
	I genuinely care about the people I work with.
	I listen carefully to understand others' points of view.
	I have good rapport with those who are impacted by the initiative.
	I have good relationships with people who need to support the project.
	Total Count for Relationships

✓	**Confidence**
	I believe this project will succeed.
	I provide others with feedback when necessary.
	I am known for speaking the truth.
	I leave meetings knowing I said what needed to be said.
	I ask for the support I need for this initiative.
	I engage in difficult conversations when the need arises.
	I take the lead in meetings.
	I am proactive, contributing before being asked.
	I believe that I can make a difference in this organization.
	I project confidence with my speech, mannerisms, posture, and dress.
	Total Count for Confidence

Summary:

Source	Count	Divide by	% Score
Authority		÷ 10	%
Expertise		÷ 8	%
Relationships		÷ 10	%
Confidence		÷ 10	%
Total		÷ 38	%

Review your responses and answer the following questions:

From which sources do you derive the most power?

How does your *level* of power affect your ability to get things done in your organization?

How do your existing *sources* of power enable you to get things done?

From which sources would you like to gain more power?

Go back over the statements that you did not mark with a check mark. For those that you would like to take action to make true, mark them with a star or asterisk (*). At the end of this chapter, you will have a chance to identify the steps you will take to increase your power.

Ways to Boost Your Organizational Power

Now that you have an idea of where you might gain more power in your organization, let's look at a few specific things you can do to boost your power.

Shore Up Your Integrity

When it comes to leading change, your integrity is your most important characteristic. If you are not credible or trustworthy, you won't earn the power needed to make change happen. When people know they can count on you, they give you the authority to take on responsibility and make decisions that affect them.

The only way to increase your integrity is to not do things that destroy it. Keep your promises, and match your actions to your words. Refrain from saying things that reduce your trustworthiness, like talking about others in their absence. Tell people the truth, even if the answer is, "I don't know." Be accessible to people in the organization, and treat others with respect. It might be helpful to partner with someone who can observe you at work and let you know when you do things that might be decreasing your integrity.

Increase Your Visibility

The more people see you and your cause for change, the more power you will have just by gaining attention. As you tap into a broader network, you will gain supporters, even detractors, but when they see you as the champion of the cause you will solidify your personal brand as a change advocate. Attention is power.

You also want leaders to take notice. To increase your visibility with them, schedule meetings, make presentations, and speak up. When management gives you their time and attention, they are giving you the opportunity to influence them. Take advantage of the power they are lending you in that moment.

Exercise the Power You Already Have

You probably have latent power that you are not using. Not using power you have is as useful as not having it at all. The following are examples of power that everyone has, but not everyone uses.

- *Time*. You exercise power by what you choose to spend your time on. You only have a finite amount of time each day, so use it wisely.
- *Knowledge*. Remember the old adage, "Knowledge is power." Share your knowledge and skills with others. Don't hoard it.
- *Attitude*. A recent study showed that happiness is contagious. You have the ability to influence others by choosing your own attitude.
- *Responsibility*. You carry power in the tasks you personally manage. Take on more responsibility, and earn more power.

When you exercise power generously, it multiplies. Advocate for others in your organization who have less power than you, and they will give it back in return.

Ask For it

In some organizations more than others, power comes from having a title. If that is the case in your organization, ask for that promotion or title change! You might just get it. At the same time, don't let not having a title be an excuse for not exercising the power you have.

Leaders can also bestow power to you by acknowledging your expertise and ownership of the project. Their attention and empowerment legitimize your efforts. If you feel like you need more support in one form or another, you might need to ask for it. Leaders may not automatically consider providing that for you, especially if it means giving up some of their own power and authority.

Review your Personal Power Inventory for those areas where you could gain more power. In the table below, list specific steps you will take to increase each of the sources of power. Then, detail what an increase in that source of power will enable you to do better or differently than today.

Power Source	Steps to Increase Power	What It Will Enable You To Do
Authority		
Expertise		
Relationships		
Confidence		

The goal of increasing your power is of course not to gain power in and of itself. Once you have more power, then it is up to you to figure out how best to use it to make change happen in your organization.

Start Conversations

Three Conversations Change Agents Must Master

Organizational change ultimately occurs one person at a time. Out of necessity to be efficient, we rely on change tools that reach multiple people at once, like meetings, training, and a host of communication methods. However, the most effective means of influencing individuals is in one-on-one conversations.

Of course, you can't have one-on-one conversations with everyone in the organization. How do you decide whom to talk to? Consider this: the most important conversations are usually the ones you would rather avoid having. If you are having a repeated conversation with someone else inside your head, then it's time to make the effort to have the talk out loud. Engaging in difficult conversations is one of the crucial skills a change agent must have to be a successful influencer.

The following are three conversations that you must be willing to start and become skilled at navigating if you want to boost your personal influence:

1. Gaining support

To implement your change initiative throughout the organization, you need the support of leaders at all levels. Starting with their initial buy-in and then their ongoing commitment and action, leaders will help drive the change in their parts of the organization.

The conversation to gain support can be daunting when you expect to have to persuade someone to get on board. You need leaders to not only believe that the change itself is worth pursuing, but also to agree that their active support is necessary to achieve the change, which can be a tall order. Adding discomfort is the fact that, as a change agent, usually you have either indirect or no authority with the leaders whose support you need. On the positive side, these conversations provide the opportunity for you to grow your influence and build momentum for your change initiative. Planning ahead goes a long way towards boosting your confidence going into the conversation.

To gain support, be clear about what their support really means — don't settle for a nod of agreement if you need them to actually do something. Align the change with their best interests. Address any concerns and show how you will help them be successful. If necessary, share stories to demonstrate the value of leadership support to change efforts.

2. Understanding resistance

When people in the organization push back, procrastinate, lay low, and do other things that seem to slow down change, we tend to experience it as resistance.

As a change agent, it can seem like resistance is something that is done to you personally. You can physically feel the drag like you are swimming upstream. It is not easy to stay neutral in a conversation when it feels like someone is pushing against you, and it can be difficult to not become defensive about the change.

When dealing with resistance, it is important to not push harder — it will only result in them pushing harder in return. Instead, realize that you are the one experiencing resistance, and they are having a normal human reaction to change. In your conversation, be curious about their experience of the change, and uncover the real reasons for their hesitation. That way, you can work with them, and not against them, to move forward.

3. Providing feedback

As people incorporate changes into their routines, you need to let them know what they are doing well and what needs improvement as they go. Feedback provides reinforcement of the change and also the opportunity for correction when necessary.

Positive feedback is usually not difficult, although it is often forgotten; negative feedback we tend to avoid giving, even when it is really needed. Not many people are comfortable sharing the news with someone that they are doing something wrong or performing ineffectively. And most people don't like hearing it, either. When you are not the recipient's boss, offering feedback can be especially difficult, because it may seem like you don't have the right to give it.

When providing feedback, start with the facts, and not your interpretation of the facts. Explain the impact of the individual's behavior or performance. Listen to the reasons without allowing excuses. Show support throughout, and maintain an attitude that you are helping them be more successful and not accusing them of wrongdoing.

When you are implementing change, it is the time to neither drop subtle hints nor to rely on mass communication to address individual issues. If you are sitting around waiting for someone to get with the change program, chances are you should talk directly with that individual. Prepare in advance and then hold a deliberate conversation to help move your initiative forward.

Although these experiences may not be entirely comfortable, you will find they are never as bad as you imagined. Taking the courageous step of having a difficult conversation will improve your self-confidence, increase respect from the other person, and result in forward progress for your initiative. With practice, you can master the ability to influence individuals through conversations.

Let's take a look at each of these conversations in more detail.

Gaining Support

Effective support for change means leaders and managers do their part to lead the change with those with whom they have authority. While you can offer guidelines for what support is needed and build mutual accountability within a larger group format, for leaders whose support is crucial to the success of the initiative, it is often a good idea to solicit their support individually, which requires a one-on-one conversation.

There are many things to consider before starting these conversations. Prepare in advance to boost your confidence and plan to get what you need. You may only get one chance to gain support, so you don't want to wing it. The following elements provide a conversation road map to help you gain support.

Desired Outcome

Determining what you want to accomplish by the end of the conversation will go a long way toward making it happen. Decide on a realistic goal for the conversation. Know what you would like the other person to commit to during the encounter. You may want agreement, or buy-in, to move forward with the initiative. You may want him to make a decision. Or, you may need him to commit to taking action or changing his own behavior. Clarify the end result so you can ensure the conversation won't end before you get what you need.

His Role

The other person will want to know how he fits into the bigger picture. Clarify his role in the change and how it relates to others who are involved. Explain why you need his unique support for the initiative. Let him know his support is not something that can be delegated. You will both boost his ego and give his personal change activities context.

Urgency

The person whose support you want will need a reason to move from his current level of support, especially if he needs to step out of his comfort zone to do so. He also needs a reason to start now. Share what will happen, to the organization and to him, if he doesn't support the initiative (or doesn't support it enough).

Benefits

If urgency communicates why he should not withhold support for change, then the benefits provide the reason he would want to support it. Share how the benefits impact him directly and indirectly. Beyond "What's in it for me," benefits cover the positive impact on the company, colleagues, customers, family and others. Share how the leader and the organization will be better off when the initiative succeeds. Connect the project and his support of it to his values.

Expectations

Support means different things to different people. Without a definition, you leave it open to interpretation, which may lead to the person doing what is comfortable instead of doing what is needed. Be specific about the support you need. Determine the activities and behaviors you expect. Understand whether these are desired or required, and how much room there is to design together how he will support the change. Identify the immediate next steps he can take to get started in the right direction.

Your Attitude

Your personal attitude toward the change is couched in how you think the other person will react to your request for support. If you go into the conversation expecting it to be a hard sell, then he might perceive your strong persuasion tactics as a lack of confidence in the project. Manage your expectation of his response to match how you think he should feel about the initiative. Do you want him to see you as enthusiastic or apologetic? Confident or hesitant? Urgent or laid back? Inviting or coercing? Choose an attitude toward the conversation and an approach that communicates what you want him to experience.

To increase support, you will most likely need to start individual conversations with leaders and others in your organization. Before you speak with them, prepare yourself with these key elements so you can be ready to bring them up to strengthen your cause and gain commitment.

Understanding Resistance

We have already discussed the importance of understanding the underlying sources of resistance you are experiencing. Through observation, you may be able to identify the key factors that are limiting support of your initiative; however, playing amateur psychologist will only take you so far. Conducting an analysis without the input of those you are analyzing puts you at risk for making incorrect assumptions. Instead, a conversation based on curiosity and respect can help uncover the real reasons for the resistance you are observing in others.

Resistance is what you feel as a change agent after telling yourself a story to interpret others' behaviors that seem to be working against the change. Ask yourself: What is an alternate story that might explain their behavior? Talk with the people going through the change to uncover what is really behind the mask of resistance. Only then can you address real concerns and design effective means of influencing change.

When sharing the plans for change along with the ideal role and behaviors with someone, you can uncover resistance by asking questions such as:

- What concerns do you have?
- What might cause this to not work?
- Which of these (if any) do you feel you could not do?
- What might stop you from doing these activities?
- What are you afraid might happen if you do these things?

The conversation to understand resistance is not a time for accusations. Instead, it should be a quest to understand the gap between your own expectations and what is actually happening.

Providing Feedback

Almost everyone can relate to having to deal with a boss or someone else in an organization who lacked self-awareness. People, especially leaders, who are oblivious to their own negative impact on colleagues derail organizational effectiveness and halt change.

As a change agent, you can't just grin and bear it. This solution creates a pressure-cooker scenario. Accepting the situation as-is does nothing to solve what is most likely a real problem that is affecting the success of your initiative. It is not going to fix itself, no matter how many subtle hints you drop.

Your only real solution is to provide feedback. Having a conversation with the person in question is the only solution that might improve the situation, even if it seems like the most difficult alternative. The following are ten tips for respectfully giving feedback to someone who is having a negative impact on your change initiative.

1. Stop the name-calling and talking behind his back about it. It only serves to destroy your own integrity, and it fuels your frustration and anger.

2. Realize that the "clueless" leader is the norm, not the outlier. The higher up in the organization someone is, the less people tell him what he doesn't want to hear. And, he doesn't realize the decrease in information.

3. Get clear about what the real issue is. If you've been working with this person for a while, chances are that everything he says is annoying. Take a step back to understand what really needs to be addressed. If it still seems like a lot of things, choose the most important. You don't want to generate a laundry list or it will seem like an attack.

4. Make sure you are in the right frame of mind for an effective conversation. Approach it with a genuine perspective that you are trying to help the person, or at least doing the best thing for the company. If you go into the conversation seeking to right a wrong or to exact some kind of revenge, not only will he be more defensive during the conversation, but it will be more awkward afterwards.

5. Plan when you will have the conversation. You don't necessarily have to schedule it, but know ahead of time for yourself when and where you will talk.

6. At the beginning of the conversation, ask permission to give the feedback. It is unlikely that he will say "no," and after saying "yes" he at least needs to hear what you have to say.

7. Unless you have permission to represent a group, don't drag other people into it. It might be comfortable to make yourself seem like one of many, but from the other person's point of view, that's a mutiny.

8. Be honest and direct. Tell him the experience from your perspective, and what the implications are. Use specific examples.

9. Expect the person to be defensive. He may deny it or even turn it around to be your own fault. Don't become defensive yourself. If you feel that you've made your case, thank him for letting you share your perspective and politely end the conversation.

10. Thank him for listening (even if it seems like he didn't). If the conversation went well, document next steps and ask how you can best follow up.

Providing feedback is difficult, especially when the recipient is higher on the org chart than you. But, your initiative hangs in the balance when people aren't doing what needs to be done. The chances are good that the person really is "clueless," and someone just needs to give him a clue. You will most likely gain respect for your honesty and courage.

Plan Ahead for a Tough Conversation

As you may have already figured out, the three types of conversations often are not exclusive. In the same conversation, you may be providing feedback about undesired behavior, understanding the resistance that drives that behavior, and trying to influence new behaviors that will demonstrate their support.

No matter the type of conversation you need to have, you can ensure a better outcome by thinking through it before it happens. That way, you can be clear about the outcome, be more confident, and have responses ready when you need it. While you can't perfectly script an effective conversation, you can determine the key points you need to discuss together. Plan ahead using the Conversation Starter Guide, which begins on the next page.

Conversation Starter Guide

Answer the following questions to prepare for your upcoming important conversation.

Who do you need to have a conversation with?

What type of conversation is it (check all that apply)?

☐ Gain support ☐ Understand resistance ☐ Give feedback ☐ Other:

What are your desired outcomes of the conversation?

What outcomes would you like to avoid?

What is the other person's role in the change?

Conversation Starter Guide

What are the benefits of the change initiative?

What will happen if the change initiative does not succeed?

What behaviors (or activities) would you like this person to stop? Provide specific examples.

What behaviors (or activities) would you like this person to start? Provide specific examples.

Conversation Starter Guide

How do you explain or interpret the current behaviors (or lack thereof)?

What are the reasonable probable causes for the current behaviors?

What impact do the current behaviors have (on him or her, the organization, the initiative, you)?

What are the personal benefits he or she will gain by changing behaviors?

Conversation Starter Guide

What questions can you ask to clarify the situation?

What attitude would you like to have going into the conversation?

When and where do you plan to have this conversation?

Break Out of the Cycle of Uncertainty

Are you still shying away from certain conversations at work because you don't know how they'll turn out? Are there questions you're avoiding asking because you don't want to know the answer?

Perhaps the actions of a leader in your organization make you doubt their commitment to the change, but instead of asking where they stand, you get frustrated by their inconsistency. Or perhaps a colleague seems to be encroaching on your area, but rather than ask, you find yourself protecting your turf. You see ambiguous events unfold, and rather than find out what's really happening, you jump to conclusions instead, and then act as if they're true.

It happens to all of us. The path we follow to get to the point where we avoid the certainty we wish we had goes something like this:

1. In the face of uncertainty, we react to events by filling in the gaps in our understanding with the worst-case scenario. Preparing for the worst possible interpretation of events allows us to protect ourselves. Unfortunately, it ends up increasing the perceived threat.

2. In light of the worst-case possibility we play in our minds, we become defensive and start building up walls around us. We interpret subsequent events in a way that supports the worst case and shuts out other, more benign possibilities.

3. Fearing the worst, we avoid finding out what's really going on. Questions that would clarify the situation go unasked, just in case what we fear is really true. It's probably not, but we'd rather not risk it. Staying in the dark only perpetuates the uncertainty.

This is the Cycle of Uncertainty, and it may be the thing that prevents your change initiative from moving forward. Take a look in the mirror – where are you not gaining clarity because you're afraid of what you'll hear? Where are you deliberately keeping yourself in the dark?

Fortunately, there are three steps you can take to break the Cycle of Uncertainty:

Check Your Assumptions
When you discover yourself avoiding asking questions because you're afraid of the answer, it's time to check your assumptions. Ask yourself: What do you know for sure? What don't you know? What assumptions have you made to fill in the gaps of your understanding? Separate the fact from the fiction.

Choose Alternate Assumptions
Once you identify the stories you've made up to try to reduce your uncertainty, you can search for an alternate story that will help you move forward. How else could you interpret the facts? What other possibilities might fill in the gaps? How would you act if they were true? Select the assumptions that help you move forward. Since you're making them up anyway, you might as well pick the ones that are enabling not disabling.

Pursue Clarity

Even with new assumptions, uncertainty is still the real problem. Armed with more positive interpretations of the situation, though, you no longer need to fear the worst. If the information exists that would reduce your uncertainty, then pursue clarity. What analysis would illuminate the real story? What questions could you ask that would reduce your uncertainty? If you can gain clarity by having a conversation, it's time to have it. In times of uncertainty, we need to build relationships, not walls.

As a change agent, it's important to recognize when you are trapped in the Cycle of Uncertainty. If you don't, you'll act out of fear instead of confidence. So, raise your awareness of being stuck in uncertainty, and choose hope over anxiety. Then, you can break the cycle by checking your assumptions, choosing alternate ones that help you move forward, and taking the steps to pursue the clarity you need.

Facilitate Meetings

In the last chapter, we addressed one-on-one conversations to influence change in individuals. Now, we will discuss how change happens through groups of people, whether they are teams, committees, working groups, or larger groups.

As you probably already know, change agents spend a lot of time in meetings. Meetings are the brunt of many office jokes, and no wonder. Professionals spend a large percentage of their time in meetings, and the higher up you are on the org chart, the more meetings you attend. A good chunk of those meetings are unnecessary, poorly run, or ineffective at making progress. As the joke goes, "I was in meetings all day, so I didn't get any work done."

In this chapter, we will look into how to use meetings effectively to drive change. We will also explore how to prevent meetings from being the place where change becomes bogged down and fizzles out.

Types of Meetings That Drive Change

First, let's look at the different types of meetings that happen in organizations as part of change efforts. Each has a different purpose and format.

Information

The information meeting is primarily a communication vehicle, where an individual or small group of people present to a larger group. They are used to share high-level concepts such as vision and strategy, updates and announcements, or recognition. Common examples are town hall meetings, corporate luncheons, and other presentations. The primary function of an information meeting is to let people know what's going on, what direction to go, and what to expect.

Information meetings take the place of more passive communication like mass emails to a large group. Instead of relying on everyone to read the message independently, the information meeting, whether in person or virtual, ensures everyone who attends hears the message at the same time. Information meetings also provide the opportunity for two-way communication through questions and answers. Information meetings take up the time of a lot of people at once, so communicators should make it worthwhile by taking advantage of the live format to set the tone for change.

Coordination

The coordination meeting is where attendees, typically team members or working groups, update each other on progress and issues that have come up since the last coordination meeting. The meeting may have a loose agenda that can be as simple as going around the room. Action happens after the coordination meeting. They are primarily used to keep everyone in the loop and on the same page. The outcomes are short-term priorities and coordination of activities and resources.

I once heard coordination meetings redundantly referred to as "team progress status update meetings." When meetings are scheduled every week for months or even years, it can start to seem like you are just going through the motions. However, coordination meetings are useful for staying focused and on track, as long as you keep an eye on the vision and goals of the change. Keep the meetings brief, perhaps standing instead of sitting. Don't get bogged down in details that not everyone in the room needs to be included in, lest they start looking at their watch. And when it starts to feel like the group is meeting just to meet, reassess the purpose, the frequency and the attendees, and switch it up a little.

Design
The design meeting is the forum for a small or medium size group to create something together. You might call it a workshop. Sample topics are mission, vision, strategy, and structural influence methods to drive change. The main activities of design meetings are creating, developing and planning. The outputs are a developed concept and an implementation plan.

Large design meetings often require a facilitator to walk the group through exercises and a process to generate ideas and develop concepts into an actionable plan. To allow the group time to create something meaningful, design meetings can last several hours to a full day or more. Design meetings are future-focused, creative, and purpose-driven.

Decision
The decision meeting is where gate keeping occurs by committee. Either someone has made a decision and needs approval by others before proceeding, or someone has come up with options for how to proceed and enlists the group to make a decision whether or which way to go. Decisions usually involve the allocation of resources or alignment to objectives. Example topics are budget allocation or which ideas to pursue. The outputs are a decision, commitment, and usually a path forward.

An effective decision meeting requires the attendance of the person or people with the proper level of authority to uphold and be accountable for the decision. All information and opinions need to get on the table so commitment is real and so the decision doesn't have to be made again when new information surfaces. Appoint advocates for all options, so the focus is on making the best decision for the organization, and not for one group getting their way over another.

Problem-Solving
In problem-solving meetings, small teams meet to solve a specific problem or improve a process. These meetings use common tools to go about analyzing the problem and coming to a solution, such as process mapping or cause-and-effect analysis. The outputs are a root cause of the problem and an improved way to operate in the future.

The emphasis in problem-solving meetings is on analysis of the current situation with the goal of developing a solution. Team members are usually those who are directly involved in the process. Help the team break out of "that's the way we've always done it" to see what is possible.

Just like with conversations, the type of meeting is usually blurred in action. Without realizing it, we drop into different modes, unaware that they require different ways of interacting.

In the next section, we will delve into the reasons that meetings become ineffective at driving change, and then we will explore how to facilitate effective meetings.

Seven Plagues that Infect Meetings

Meetings bear the brunt of a lot of ire, with good reason. Meetings are relied on as the main means of working together, even though meetings are often rife with obstacles that slow progress and hinder change.

The following are seven challenges that can plague a meeting, and what you can do to avoid them.

Meeting is Unnecessary

Meetings have become the default means of working with other people. Sometimes meetings are called out of habit, when other methods of communication would suffice. Meetings that don't need to happen are a waste of time and interrupt the work that people were doing outside the conference room. Hosting unnecessary meetings communicates that you think your time is more valuable than that of everyone attending. Instead of creating excitement about the project, you end up generating resentment and boredom.

In this day and age, there are a number of internet-based tools that can easily share information and help coordinate activities. Knowledge management systems, project management programs, videos and even email are all examples of tools that can replace the need for some meetings. The trick is instilling the discipline to regularly update and refer to these systems instead of waiting for a meeting and counting on the transfer to happen in person.

Sometimes a part of the meeting is unnecessary. People figure while everyone is together, they might as well talk about other topics. Piling on agenda items results in covering too much in the meeting, making it difficult to focus.

Before you schedule a meeting, challenge yourself to find alternate means of connecting that don't require everyone to meet at the same time. Meetings should only include that which must be done together. Information should only be shared in person if the meaning would be lost via other communication vehicles. Any task that can be done independently and asynchronously should be done that way.

No Clear Purpose or Agenda

The purpose of a meeting serves as the beacon, the reason for meeting. The agenda provides the flow of the conversation that enables the purpose to happen. For a meeting to be most effective, the purpose and the agenda must be clear.

When the purpose of the meeting is not clearly stated, each person joins the conversation with his own preconceived purpose for attending the meeting, if he has one at all. Without a clear outcome and output, you can end up leaving the meeting without having accomplished what was needed.

Keeping the desired outcome in mind, the agenda walks attendees through the steps to get to that point. Estimated times for each topic allows you to keep the meeting on track. Without an agenda, it is easy to go off on tangents, and just talk until time runs out (or beyond).

Determine what you need the group to accomplish by the end of their limited time together. Identify the key outputs of the meeting — decisions, discussions, creations, priorities, etc. Design the meeting with the required steps and final outcomes in mind. Then create an agenda that helps the meeting flow and stay on time.

Wrong People in the Room
Often, meetings have too many people, too few people, or the wrong individuals in the room for the task at hand. As a result, meetings get bogged down, make faulty progress, or end up needing to meet again with different people.

Too many people in the room can create chaos from too many voices needing to be corralled. People who don't really need to be there get bored. However, it's easy for too many people to be invited to a meeting. Some meeting planners follow a "the more the merrier" philosophy when sending out invitations. Others invite people who don't need to be there because they don't want someone to get mad or have hurt feelings for not being included. Inviting people to a meeting can seem like the easiest way to get their buy-in and involvement. Unfortunately, crowded meetings tend to get bogged down because everyone feels the need to participate.

On the other side of the spectrum, having too few attendees limits the points of view and could mean that the group is not hearing key information. Sometimes people don't get invited who should be at the meeting. Some are simply forgotten. Sometimes organizational hierarchy can get in the way, leaving out people because they are too high or too low on the org chart based on the other people in the room. Some people are invited and either can't attend or decide not to show up, leaving the group shorthanded. When groups are missing people, they are missing information and opinions that they need to make the best progress possible.

Sometimes meetings can have the wrong people. Friends are invited instead of people who have the most knowledge. Some attendees don't get along, and their relationship holds back the team. Others don't want to be there and fail to participate. Decision meetings especially can suffer when the person with the right level of authority does not attend. Meetings with the wrong people usually require a do-over with the right people.

When selecting the people to invite to the meeting, choose wisely. The number of people should be enough to provide a good mix of perspectives and knowledge, while still having few enough to have a manageable conversation. Ensure you have the right level of authority for any decisions that will be made. No one should be invited who is unable to actively contribute to the desired outcome.

Lack of Participation

Sometimes you have the right people in the room, but the real conversation that needs to take place doesn't happen. Meeting attendees censor themselves, resulting in a lack of ideas, opinions, constructive disagreement, and differing points of view.

One leading cause of people not speaking up in meetings is fear. Fear of being wrong, fear of retribution, and fear of looking foolish are a few. Leaders frequently and inadvertently squelch candor just by their mere presence in the room because authority heightens fear.

Another reason for silence or easy agreement is not wanting to cause conflict. Effective meetings require a dose of healthy disagreement, which means attendees vet differing ideas and opinions without attacking each other personally and harming their relationships. Conflict is often avoided in the name of team spirit. Conflict avoidance also has its roots in a lack of trust amongst team members, since open sharing and disagreement requires a level of individual vulnerability to the group.

When people are not fully participating, it is best to address it directly. Work first behind the scenes with individuals to assess the reason for lack of participation, and then take steps to remove those reasons when the group is together.

People Come Unprepared

We've already joked that real work doesn't happen in meetings, and yet so many people don't do the work that is required between meetings! Minutes and updates are sent and people don't read them. People have tasks assigned that don't get completed.

When people show up to meetings unprepared, then meeting time is spent catching them up. This redundancy causes resentment amongst those who actually did come prepared, and in turn makes them want to come unprepared to the next meeting.

When people don't do their homework between meetings, then progress halts. The success of the team relies on members doing their part. Meeting when someone has not completed their tasks wastes the other members' time.

Ensure attendees come to your meetings prepared through a combination of hand-holding and accountability. Check in with people between meetings to make sure they know what is expected of them and to see how they are making progress. If they are struggling to complete their homework, you can then learn why and help them if necessary. Send reminders so items don't get lost in the day to day work. At the meeting, conduct a check-in to verify that everyone is prepared and has done the tasks they committed to doing.

Switching Formats

Each of the meeting formats described in the last section require different approaches and modes of interacting. Meetings that switch formats without switching modes can be frustrating for attendees.

For example, design meetings require a creative, open mindset, while decision meetings require judgment. When judgment is applied in the midst of a design meeting, it shuts down the flow of ideas and makes people defensive. Likewise, when a design mindset is applied when a decision is required, all the options and "what-ifs" prevent drawing the conversation to a confident decision.

After determining the outcomes of the meeting, decide which type of meeting will work best. If the path to reach the outcome requires more than one type of meeting, then separate the meeting into sections so you can design the best approach to each individually. Schedule breaks between the sections and plan to introduce the new way the group will interact for each.

The Meeting Protects the Status Quo

Meetings are one of the main ways organizational resistance is reinforced. In that way, the meeting itself can contribute to a lack of change.

Put a bunch of people in a room and they adopt unspoken rules for how to work together: how they should treat each other, what ideas and behaviors are acceptable, and what topics are important or taboo. If you don't change the way people interact in meetings, you most likely will not see change in the organization.

Pay attention to the places where the group seems to get stuck. Identify the behaviors that are preventing the team from moving forward. Then, for the sake of your change initiative, take a step back and address the behaviors with the group. Agree on the new way of working together and then be deliberate and diligent in holding the group accountable.

Additional Tips for Facilitating Productive Meetings

As a change agent, whether you lead or participate, you will most likely need to step forward to facilitate meetings to drive your change initiative forward. Besides avoiding the plagues, follow these tips to increase the productivity of your meetings, and thus make progress on your change initiative.

Prepare in Advance

At a bare minimum, create and distribute the agenda and any review materials beforehand. To be most effective, meet with individual team members before the meeting to prepare them for what is expected of them. Leave only the key items that need to be done together for the meeting agenda. Everything else should be done in advance to the extent possible.

Agree on Ground Rules

People don't automatically know how to relate to one another in a meeting. To set the stage, declare ground rules that the group will abide by during the meeting. Select ground rules that will help mold how they should interact based on the type of meeting it is. Invite attendees to add their own ground rules based on the concerns they have about working together. Then gain agreement on the ground rules, and refer to them when someone in the group strays.

Start and End on Time

When you start and end on time, you respect the time of the people at the meeting, and you also demonstrate commitment to your initiative. Start on time, regardless of who is missing. That way, you show respect to those who are on time instead of those who are late. End on time or even a few minutes early, because once the clock goes beyond the end time, people start paying more attention to the clock than to the task at hand. If the outcomes have not been achieved, and you must stay beyond the scheduled time, acknowledge the predicament and ask for permission to continue.

Establish the Facilitator Role

The role of meeting facilitator, whether you take it on yourself or assign it to someone else, is a critical function that should be done in awareness and acknowledgment of the rest of the meeting participants. The facilitator monitors team dynamics, maintains the ground rules, and works to improve interactions. He helps keep the meeting on track with the agenda by reeling in runaway conversations. He ensures the meeting doesn't inadvertently switch formats. And he watches for ways the meeting inhibits making progress on the change itself and calls it out.

Integrate fun

A stodgy conference room needs a jolt of energy to break its inhabitants out of their normal habits. Sometimes the air is thick with politics. Play and humor are great equalizers. Use creativity toys, games and role-playing to break the tension, kick people out of their comfort zones and get your point across. When you take charge as a facilitator, you will be surprised what people will do if you tell them to, regardless of their title.

One way to increase support for your change initiative is to not make people dread getting together to talk about it. When you follow these rules and avoid the seven plagues, meetings will start to be meaningful and productive, and even enjoyable.

Pre-Meeting Checklist and Post-Meeting Assessment

I have emphasized the importance of preparing in advance. The tools on the following pages will help you.

The Meeting Checklist helps you prepare for your next important meeting. At the top, start with the date, location, and general topic for the meeting. List the desired outcomes, plus any outputs that will be created during the meeting. Check the box with the appropriate meeting type(s). Under agenda, detail the items to be discussed and the allotted time for each, then list the attendees. Based on the type of meeting, identify the appropriate ground rules that will allow for the required mindset. Next, list any work that must be done in preparation for the meeting, either by yourself or by attendees. While the Pre-Meeting Checklist is a valuable preparation tool for you, it can also be used to communicate details about the meeting with the attendees.

The Post-Assessment enables you to grade how it went afterwards, so you can find areas to improve upon for the next meeting. Rate the statements on a scale from 1 to 5, with 5 meaning you strongly agree and 1 meaning you strongly disagree. Add comments for what should be addressed during the next meeting. Invite the attendees to complete the assessment as well, so you get a fuller picture of how the meeting went and how to improve future meetings.

Pre-Meeting Checklist

Date: **Topic:** **Location:**

Desired Outcomes and Outputs

Meeting Type (Check all that apply)

☐ Information   ☐ Coordination   ☐ Design   ☐ Decision   ☐ Problem-Solving

Agenda	Attendees

Proposed Ground Rules	Prep Work

Post-Meeting Assessment

Date:　　　　　　　　**Topic:**

Indicate the degree to which you agree (5=Strongly Agree, 1=Strongly Disagree) with the following statements. Then add comments about what to improve upon next time the group meets.

Factor	Rating:	What should be addressed next time?
Attendees participated	☐1 ☐2 ☐3 ☐4 ☐5	
Desired outcome was achieved	☐1 ☐2 ☐3 ☐4 ☐5	
Agenda was followed	☐1 ☐2 ☐3 ☐4 ☐5	
Attendees came prepared	☐1 ☐2 ☐3 ☐4 ☐5	
Ground rules were followed	☐1 ☐2 ☐3 ☐4 ☐5	
Meeting started and ended on time	☐1 ☐2 ☐3 ☐4 ☐5	

The Case for Courage

Being a change agent is not for the faint of heart. You often have to deliberately step into uncomfortable situations without knowing how they will turn out. For example, you may need to:

- Force people to slow down and think about the impact of change, when they would rather just get it done.
- Provide feedback to those with whom you have no direct authority.
- Get people talking about awkward or difficult topics, and make them interact in ways they aren't used to doing.
- Enlist the support you need, even when people don't like the project.
- Add more workload to already busy schedules.
- Make people feel dissatisfied with the results they've achieved so far and the work they've done to get the organization to the current state.
- Get people to acknowledge and eliminate the subtle ways they undermine change.
- Overstep the usual bounds of your own authority to find out where the line really is.

Your responsibility as change agent is to help the organization fully realize the desired results of the project. Your task is to bring the rest of the organization with you to a new destination. To do that, they have to break out of doing business as usual.

If you want people to stop doing business as usual, then by definition you must introduce something unusual. You have to do things that people in your organization don't usually do, and get others to follow along. If you want people to step out of their comfort zones, then you must be willing to step out of your own.

To avoid discomfort, we often tell ourselves the barriers to change are unchangeable, so we don't have to try: Managers can't lead. People resist change. Everyone is too busy. It is what it is. But look a little deeper and we find the truth: we're not willing to do the things that give the project a chance to succeed. When we hit that brick wall and can see that the change initiative is stuck, our fear can blind us to the possibility that there is an option beyond accepting things the way they are.

The whole point of being a change agent is doing the things that will make change happen – even when they are risky, uncomfortable, or difficult. What uncomfortable, scary thing could you do that might give your project a chance to succeed? What would you do if not doing it meant that your project would surely fail? If there are answers to these questions, then surely you have an obligation to try them.

To be the best change agent you can be, step out in courage and embrace the discomfort as part of the job. Do it because no one else will do it. If not you, then who?

"You must do the thing you think you cannot do." ~ Eleanor Roosevelt

Appendix

Final Thoughts

The Dance of Change

Despite our better intentions, changing organizations is never predictable, and doesn't perfectly fit into a nice theoretical model the way we wish it would.

As change agents, we frequently dance in the moment. While we work toward an envisioned future, we can only handle what is right in front of us, which is constantly shifting based on the reactions to the strategies we are using to try to influence change. We must be experts at both designing change and at handling what to do when it doesn't work the way we intended. Having completed this workbook, you now have the tools that will enable you to become an *Irresistible* change agent who implements *Irresistible* change.

I would love to hear your success stories and invite you to email them to me. For further assistance as you design and influence change, please contact me and I will be happy to point you towards the resources that will best suit your needs. You may also find information about additional resources, including workshops, training, and coaching, at www.enclaria.com.

Best wishes for your change initiative,

Heather Stagl

Enclaria LLC
(678) 644-2886
heather@enclaria.com

Index of Templates

Template	Page
Status Quo Inventory	8
Future State Outlook	20
Before And After Chart	27
Layers of Change Analysis	30
Change Impact Assessment	34
Force Field Analysis	36
Plan for Resistance Chart	47
Individual Resistance Assessment	49
Roles and Relationships Diagram	67
Leadership Support Chart	75
Structural Influence Chart	91
Initiative Scorecard	99
Accountability Agreement	104
Communication Plan	119
Personal Influence Chart	127
Personal Power Inventory	133
Conversation Starter Guide	145
Pre-Meeting Checklist	158
Post-Meeting Assessment	159

Resistance and *99 Ways to Influence Change*

In 2010, I published a book called *99 Ways to Influence Change*. It is a great companion to this workbook. Here is the list of the *99 Ways* sorted by the source of resistance it reduces.

Valid Concerns
20. Remove obstacles
33. Listen
50. Address objections
66. Respect resistance
70. Be flexible
72. Be patient

Information
1. Tell stories
9. Clarify expectations
10. Provide feedback
15. Start conversations
19. Make it viral
29. Reframe it
36. Prioritize
49. Point to the destination
60. Identify key behaviors
62. Share what works
71. Measure progress
76. Recognize success
83. Increase awareness
92. Set clear goals
98. Communicate

Skills
38. Educate
40. Build new skills
46. Provide useful tools
84. Install new habits

Motivation
4. Say "please"
6. Ridicule
7. Generate scarcity
11. Establish urgency
16. Demand compliance
21. Show others are doing it
25. Rely on friends
26. Beg
27. Instigate competition
28. Instill curiosity
31. Set the default
34. Bribe
35. Encourage
37. Give praise
41. Do favors
51. Drop names
52. Celebrate success
53. Connect to values
54. Say "thank you"
57. Find the emotion
58. Ask for help
59. Incite a riot
64. Hold them accountable
65. Induce guilt
68. Gain commitment
69. Make it fun
77. Generate short-term wins
79. Flatter
81. Nag
85. Threaten
86. Assign responsibility
90. Establish deadlines
93. Entertain
94. Incorporate into identity
97. Harness peer pressure
99. Offer incentives

Power
3. Involve them
8. Transfer ownership
23. Ask for ideas
47. Join forces
56. Extend an invitation
75. Get leadership support
80. Empower
88. Share in the design
95. Design choices

Fear
5. Allow failure
13. Acknowledge fears
17. Develop support systems
39. Help them succeed
45. Laugh about it
61. Keep it simple
67. Go there first
73. Shrink it
82. Enlist early adopters
89. Reduce risk
91. Foster resilience

Trust
2. Model behavior
14. Show you care
18. Admit mistakes
22. Tell the truth
32. Build trust
43. Keep promises
44. Remove doubt
48. Remove dead weight
55. Be consistent
74. Establish authority
87. Build relationships
96. Show respect

Resources
12. Remove enablers
24. Make it easy
30. Facilitate meetings
42. Fix problems
63. Adjust the environment
78. Eliminate noise

The Levers of Influence and *99 Ways to Influence Change*

Here is the list from *99 Ways to Influence Change* sorted by the five fundamental levers of influence.

Provide Clarity
1. Tell stories
2. Model behavior
9. Clarify expectations
10. Provide feedback
22. Tell the truth
29. Reframe it
36. Prioritize
49. Point to the destination
60. Identify key behaviors
61. Keep it simple
62. Share what works
71. Measure progress
76. Recognize success
83. Increase awareness
90. Establish deadlines
92. Set clear goals
98. Communicate

Enable Progress
5. Allow failure
12. Remove enablers
13. Acknowledge fears
17. Develop support systems
20. Remove obstacles
24. Make it easy
30. Facilitate meetings
31. Set the default
38. Educate
39. Help them succeed
40. Build new skills
46. Provide useful tools
48. Remove dead weight
63. Adjust the environment
73. Shrink it
78. Eliminate noise
84. Install new habits
91. Foster resilience

95. Design choices

Build Trust
4. Say "please"
14. Show you care
18. Admit mistakes
32. Build trust
33. Listen
41. Do favors
42. Fix problems
43. Keep promises
44. Remove doubt
45. Laugh about it
50. Address objections
54. Say "thank you"
55. Be consistent
66. Respect resistance
67. Go there first
70. Be flexible
72. Be patient
74. Establish authority
77. Generate short-term wins
87. Build relationships
89. Reduce risk
96. Show respect

Invite Participation
3. Involve them
8. Transfer ownership
15. Start conversations
19. Make it viral
23. Ask for ideas
25. Rely on friends
47. Join forces
56. Extend an invitation
59. Ask for help
68. Gain commitment
75. Get leadership support
80. Empower

82. Enlist early adopters
86. Assign responsibility
88. Share in the design

Motivate Action
6. Ridicule
7. Generate scarcity
11. Establish urgency
16. Demand compliance
21. Show others are doing it
26. Beg
27. Instigate competition
28. Instill curiosity
34. Bribe
35. Encourage
37. Give praise
51. Drop names
52. Celebrate success
53. Connect to values
57. Find the emotion
58. Incite a riot
64. Hold them accountable
65. Induce guilt
69. Make it fun
79. Flatter
81. Nag
85. Threaten
93. Entertain
94. Incorporate into identity
97. Harness peer pressure
99. Offer incentives

Irresistible Change Guide

About the Author

Heather Stagl

As change management coach and founder of Enclaria LLC, since 2009, Heather Stagl has partnered with individuals and teams to help them become effective change agents for their organizations. She has seventeen years of team facilitation and training experience and spent three years as the Director of Organizational Effectiveness at a mid-size food products manufacturer. More recently, she conducted an extensive executive training program on strategy execution at Balanced Scorecard Collaborative. She holds a Bachelor of Science in Industrial Engineering from Northwestern University and an MBA in Leadership and Change Management from DePaul University. Heather completed coaching training at The Coaches Training Institute.

Printed in Great Britain
by Amazon.co.uk, Ltd.,
Marston Gate.